Coopers &Lybrand

Analysis:
1997 Tax Legislation

August 1997   Third Printing

President Clinton has announced that he will sign the Tax Relief Act of 1997 into law on August 5, 1997. This date is referred to as the "date of enactment" throughout this publication.

Contents

Tables, Graphs, Charts and Examples

Introduction

The "Revenue Reconciliation Act of 1997," also known as the "Tax Relief Act of 1997," is the culmination of campaign promises that began with President Clinton's election in 1992 and the Republican sweep of Congressional seats in 1994. It marries the twin objectives of balancing the federal budget and reducing taxes. Those who claim paternity hope it will balance the budget by 2002 and, for more than one moment in time, reduce taxes on middle-income families, provide stimulus for continued economic growth and investment by reducing taxes on capital gains, estates and savings, make college more affordable for all and redress a number of other ills in the current tax Code. The U.S. House of Representatives and Senate passed the Act on July 31, 1997, and President Clinton announced that he would sign the bill on August 5, 1997.

President Clinton campaigned in 1992 and again in 1996 on a very broad agenda, but each campaign included middle-income tax relief and the priority of investment in the future, especially education and the environment. After the 1992 election, his advisors persuaded him to put balancing the budget first. As a result, the Omnibus Reconciliation Act of 1993 was primarily a tax-increase and spending-cut bill that now seems to be producing a much more manageable budget deficit than expected. But the 1993 Act was hard to swallow, and the Republicans campaigned hard in 1994 on the need to finish the job on the spending side and provide needed tax relief for all income groups, investors and small businesses. Their "Contract with America," credited with the Republican sweep in the 1994 Congressional elections, contained many of the themes we now see embodied in the 1997 tax act, after a partisan effort in 1995 drew a Presidential veto.

The first steps toward the difficult compromises that were necessary to produce this bill were evident in the re-election of President Clinton and of a Republican Congress in the fall of 1996. The 1996 elections produced a consensus of sorts—the President endorsed the priority of balancing the federal budget and agreed to the Republican demand for tax cuts as part of the equation. While the President stressed again that, in his view, the first claim on tax relief was held by middle-income working families, the Republican Congress has been equally steadfast in its demand for reduced taxes on capital gains, estates and savings as part of the agenda for continued economic growth. Melding these competing objectives into one bill that also purports to balance the budget has challenged the political skills of all participants. It was accomplished by the political imperative felt by each side that they had to deliver what they had promised to the voters.

Ultimately, the budget package produced is slated to reduce spending over the next five years by $270 billion and taxes by a net $95 billion (consisting of gross tax cuts of $151 billion, offset by $56 billion in revenue increases). Both the gross and net tax numbers exceed those in the initial budget agreement. Whether the 1997 Act delivers on its promise to balance the budget by 2002 and contains out-year costs remains to be seen. There was minimal effort to deal with the thorny issues causing the budget's expected imbalance in the next century. No reform of entitlement programs was achieved, despite attempts by Senate Republicans and exhortations by budget experts that the sooner the better in order to minimize the needed changes. Opponents of the tax relief component of the bill argue that the future costs of several provisions promise to explode and will undermine any ability to balance the budget after these office-holders are gone. Of special concern in this regard are the capital gains and estate tax relief and back-loaded IRAs. In addition, the bill creates new entitlements in the tax code—the education and child care credits—and new spending program for child health care. Other analysts are disappointed in the large number of special interest items, the complexity and administrative difficulty of many provisions, especially those targeted at aver-

Coopers & Lybrand L.L.P.

age taxpayers, and the absence of more reform in areas of the Code that are quite troublesome today, such as international tax rules and the alternative minimum tax for individuals and corporations. Taken together, these sentiments seem destined to insure that tax legislation stays on the agenda well into the next century.

Outlook

The performance of the economy is arguably the most important factor to watch in assessing the success of the 1997 Act in accomplishing its dual purpose and thus the need for Congress and the President to revisit this agenda in the near term. Strong growth will propel us toward a better fiscal equation, while weak or moderate growth will exacerbate any missed targets on both the spending and revenue sides. Of course, as always, many estimates will not prove out, and some could be widely off the mark. Predicting capital asset sales and IRA savings behavior is notably difficult, and factors outside the tax system are paramount.

Similarly, such external factors as the rate of growth in the costs of medical care and education, the aging of the population and the rate of income growth are expected to force Congress and the President to seriously revamp entitlement programs funded by the federal government within the next few years. These efforts are likely to implicate the tax system, and we predict a continued atmosphere of incremental tax change. There is an outside chance that external forces may require an extensive and more serious effort at tax simplification within our present structure.

As for tax reform, the future occupant of the White House will be the most instrumental figure in determining whether a dramatic change in our tax system becomes an agenda item. Although there is widespread dislike for what we have, consensus on changing it is hard to come by, and the number of winners and losers has to be daunting for all but the most committed politician. Members of the House GOP leadership plan a concerted effort in the fall of 1997, looking forward to the next elections, to educate the voters about what is at stake. The success of these efforts will be determinative in the short run, but other factors may ultimately be more important. For example, the ability of the IRS to "reform" itself and modernize its operations may persuade future Administrations about the best direction to head with our tax system. The international issues being faced by the United States, Europe and other countries with regard to energy and environmental taxes could influence the shape of our future tax system. And, as always, the search for the magic economic bullet will continue.

Provisions Subject to the Line-Item Veto

Under current law, Congress has granted the President yet-untested line-item veto authority against certain new direct spending and limited tax benefits. The Joint Committee on Taxation is required to submit to the Conference Committee on all tax legislation a list of limited tax benefits. The Conferees must then determine whether to include the Joint Committee's statement in the Conference Report.

Failure to include the Joint Committee's statement in the Conference Report passes to the President the authority to determine which provisions provide limited tax benefits subject to line-item veto authority. Inclusion of this statement limits the President's authority to canceling only one or more of these provisions so identified as limited tax benefits.

The bill submitted to President Clinton does include a list of 79 separate provisions identified as "limited tax benefits" by the Joint Committee on Taxation. It is not known whether President Clinton will opt to exercise his line-item veto authority against any of these proposals. This list ranges from provisions extending the research and experimentation tax credit to a provision lowering the alcohol excise tax on certain hard ciders. Other examples of limited tax benefits include the provision relating to the deduction for contributions of appreciated stock to a private foundation and the provision granting foreign sales corporation benefits to software makers.

* * * * *

Given the broad-based, high tax rate structure of our income tax, laced with special incentives and targeted benefits, it will be imperative for all taxpay-

Coopers & Lybrand L.L.P.

ers—even those of more modest means—and all businesses to stay abreast of those provisions that may benefit them in order to plan their economic affairs as creatively and prudently as possible.

This publication provides an overview of the principal tax elements of the 1997 Act. The "observations," examples, graphs and tables throughout the text offer our analysis of the implications of the provisions to businesses and individuals. Effective dates of any tax law changes are noted to assist in determining effects and in tax planning.

The skilled professionals of Coopers & Lybrand, who have followed closely the legislative developments of the new law, welcome the opportunity to assist you with analyzing the Act and its effects on your affairs, as well as in planning to take advantage of its opportunities and to minimize any potentially adverse consequences of its various provisions.

Individuals

The new law creates a patchwork of tax breaks for middle- and upper-income families. Families receive certain benefits, and, in addition, may need to choose among several investment options. Complex analysis may be required to determine the best course of action.

Simply stated, in 1998, a middle-income family (one with adjusted gross income of $60,000) may benefit from the following:

❑ $400 tax credit for each child under age 17;
❑ an education credit for children in college;
❑ the ability to withdraw existing IRA funds to pay college expenses without the early withdrawal penalty;
❑ choices among new tax-favored investment vehicles, such as education IRAs, back-loaded "Roth IRAs," as well as more liberalized rules for traditional IRAs;
❑ more favorable treatment of qualified state prepaid tuition trusts.

This array of benefits is subject to varying phaseouts and eligibility requirements. A tremendous education process will be required to fully inform middle-income families about the specific benefits. Set forth below are the rules for each provision.

Family Tax Relief

Child Tax Credit

The new law provides qualifying families with a tax credit for each child under age 17 as of the close of the tax year. The credit amount will be $400 in 1998 and $500 thereafter. A child is eligible if he or she can be claimed as a dependent and is a son or daughter, or is a direct descendent, stepchild or foster child of the taxpayer.

> **Observation:** Both political parties have advocated some type of "middle class" tax relief for several years. The child or family tax credit was the centerpiece of the House Republican "Contract with America" tax package advanced in 1994. Such relief is designed to address a family's reduced ability to pay taxes as family size increases. Congressional staff estimate that the value of the dependent personal exemption has declined in real terms by over one-third over the last 50 years.

> **Observation:** The revenue cost of the child credit provisions is in excess of $85 billion over five years, representing almost three-fifths of the tax cuts in the revenue reconciliation package.

The amount of the total child tax credit would be reduced beginning at $110,000 of modified adjusted gross income (MAGI) for married couples filing jointly, $75,000 for individuals and heads of household, and $55,000 for

Coopers & Lybrand L.L.P.

married couples filing separately. The reduction occurs at the rate of $50 for each $1,000 (or portion thereof) of MAGI above the threshold. For example, a couple with one child and $115,000 of MAGI would have their credit reduced by $250 ($5,000/$1,000 X $50).

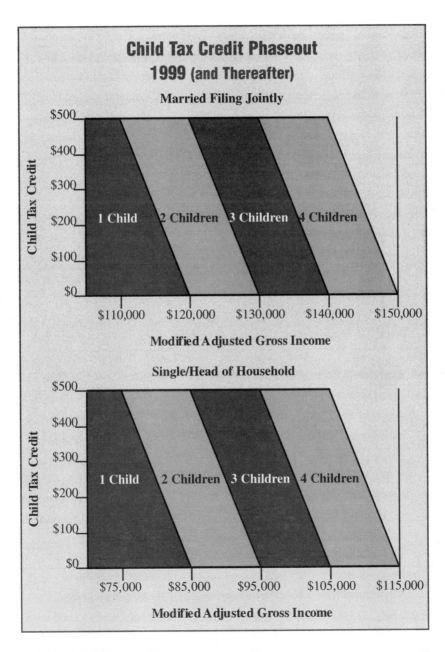

Observation: When fully effective in 1999, the amount of the child credit will be subject to complete phaseout for each $10,000 of MAGI over the $110,000 threshold amount ($120,000 for married families filing jointly with one child, $130,000 if they have two qualified children, etc.).

As a political compromise to address questions of whether certain low- and middle-income families will receive any benefits from the child tax credit in cases where the earned income tax credit already reduces regular tax liability, the new law includes a complex formula to provide certain large families (those with three or more qualifying children) with a refund of a portion of the employee share of payroll taxes paid. The new law provides that families with three or more children can receive a refund of a portion of payroll taxes in cases where the earned income tax credit (EITC) and the child tax credit would already eliminate regular tax liability.

The following hypothetical example illustrates the benefits of the child credit for low-income families:

Family with MAGI of $23,000:

Taxes		Credits	
Income taxes before EITC	$675	EITC	$1,668
Payroll taxes			
(employee share)	1,760	Child credit	767*
Total	$2,435	Total	$2,435

(Assumes EITC and tax figures released by the White House.)
Note: Benefit from child credit is limited.

Observation: The added revenue cost of extending the child credit to lower-income families will be paid for by tightening the eligibility requirements and fraud detection provisions governing the EITC.

Education Incentives

The new law contains several significant education incentives designed to assist families to pay for the costs of education, principally at the post-secondary level. The Clinton Administration has advocated reducing the after-tax cost of education to encourage investment in education and training, targeting such benefits to middle-income families. One of the major thrusts of the tax incentives is to make 14 years of education (including the first 2 post-secondary years) the norm in America.

Education Incentives: Summary

Incentive	Provision	Eligibility
Post-secondary education tax credits (HOPE Scholarship for first and second year, lifetime learning for others)	Allows tax credits of $1,500 for the first 2 years of qualified higher education expenses with additional credits ($1,000/$2,000) for later qualified education.	Credit phased out for single filers at $50,000 MAGI and for married filing joint at $100,000.
Education savings incentives	Expands benefits from state prepaid tuition trusts and excludes from income distributions of untaxed income from education IRAs.	No MAGI limit for tuition trusts; education IRA contributions phased out for married filing joint at $160,000 MAGI.
Student loan interest deduction	Allows above-the-line deduction for qualified interest on student loans.	Phased out for single at $55,000 MAGI, married at $75,000.

IRA withdrawals for education	Waives 10% penalty on early withdrawals from IRAs for distributions used for qualified higher education expenses.	Limited to qualified education expenses; taxable if regular IRA; tax-free for Roth IRA.
Income exclusion for employer-provided education	Extends present law exclusion for courses beginning before June 1, 2000.	Limitation remains $5,250 of education expenses for undergraduate courses only.

Higher Education Tax Credits

The new law provides a nonrefundable HOPE Scholarship tax credit for qualified tuition and fees (but not the cost of room and board or books) for the first two years of post-secondary education in a degree or certificate program. For these two years, the credit is allowed at a rate of 100 percent of the first $1,000 and 50 percent of the next $1,000 of qualified education expenses during any academic period beginning in the tax year.

> **Observation:** The credit will be available for the tax year in which the expenses are paid as long as the education begins or continues during that year or begins during the first three months of the next year. The HOPE Scholarship credit is available for only the first two years of post-secondary education, and students who have completed those years will not be eligible for the credit.

The new law also provides a Lifetime Learning tax credit of up to 20 percent of $5,000 ($10,000 for tax years beginning in 2003) of qualified tuition and fees (but not the cost of room and board or books) paid during the tax year. Individuals will not be eligible for the Lifetime Learning tax credit in any year in which they claim the HOPE Scholarship tax credit.

In contrast to the HOPE Scholarship credit, the Lifetime Learning credit may be claimed for an unlimited number of years. Thus, the Lifetime Learning credit can be used for graduate or other professional degree education. The credit is available for any course of instruction at an eligible educational institution if the student acquires or improves job skills.

Both the HOPE Scholarship and the Lifetime Learning tax credits will phase out ratably for those with modified adjusted gross income between $40,000 and $50,000 ($80,000 and $100,000 for joint returns).

> **Observation:** The coordination of the two credits could provide eligible families with tax credits for four years of undergraduate education, as summarized in the chart below.

Higher Education Tax Credits

College Year	Amount of Tuition Allowed	Percentage of Tuition	Max. Allowable Credit
1	$1,000	100%	
	$1,000	50%	$1,500
2	$1,000	100%	
	$1,000	50%	$1,500
3	$5,000	20%	$1,000
4	$5,000	20%	$1,000

> **Observation:** The HOPE credit is weighted so that families with qualified part-time students or those with lower tuition or fees are more likely to cover all of their education costs with the credit. For example, the $1,500 credit limit is almost $300 above the national average community college tuition and would make such education "tuition-free" for over two-thirds of all community college students.

Qualified tuition expenses paid with loan proceeds generally will be eligible for the HOPE scholarship credit immediately—rather than waiting until the loan is repaid. The credit amount will be recaptured if the student receives a refund of tuition or other qualified expense for which a credit was claimed in prior years.

> **Observation:** Scholarships, fellowships or other payments that are not included in income, such as employer-provided education assistance, will not be considered qualified tuition expenses. Tuition paid with the proceeds of a gift or inheritance would, however, qualify for the HOPE Scholarship credit.

Students eligible for the HOPE Scholarship credit must carry at least one-half the normal full-time work load for one academic period during the tax year and must have earned a high school diploma or equivalent degree. In contrast, the Lifetime Learning credit is available for students enrolled less than half-time.

> **Observation:** The new law does not require that an eligible student maintain at least a B– grade in order to be eligible for the credit—as once proposed by the Clinton Administration.

Students claimed as dependents may not claim either the HOPE Scholarship credit or the Lifetime Learning credit on their own return. Parents who claim the students as dependents may treat any qualified tuition or related expenses paid by the student as paid by the parent in determining the amount of their credit.

The IRS will issue regulations providing appropriate rules for record-keeping and information reporting that will address the information reports that eligible educational institutions will be required to file to assist students and the IRS in calculating the amount of the HOPE Scholarship credit and Lifetime Learning credit potentially available.

The Hope Scholarship credit applies to expenses paid after December 31, 1997, for education furnished after that date. The Lifetime Learning credit applies to expenses paid after June 30, 1998, for education furnished after that date.

Qualified State Prepaid Tuition Programs

The 1996 tax law granted tax-exempt status to qualified state prepaid tuition programs that permit individuals to either purchase tuition credits for individuals or make contributions to accounts established for meeting the education expenses of the account beneficiary. Distributions from these accounts are included in income only to the extent that the amounts exceed contributions made on behalf of the beneficiary, or the contributor, such as a parent, receives a refund exceeding contributions made by that person. Amounts distributed from qualified state prepaid tuition programs generally will be included in income in the same manner as present law rules governing annuities.

The new law makes several changes to the provisions governing qualified state prepaid tuition programs. The most important change provides that qualified expenses now include room and board, as well as tuition, fees, books and supplies.

As under present law, no earnings from a qualified state prepaid tuition program are included in the income of the contributor to or the beneficiary of the program until a distribution is made from the program. At that time, the earnings portion of the distribution will be included in the income of the distributee. However, if the distributions are used to pay qualified education expenses, the distributee or parent can still claim the HOPE Scholarship credit or Lifetime Learning credit if the other requirements for these credits are satisfied, including the adjusted gross income limitations.

The inclusion of room and board expenses as qualified higher education expenses is effective for tax years ending after August 20, 1996.

Education IRAs

The new law also provides an income exclusion for amounts distributed from an education individual retirement account (IRA), a trust or a custodial account created by qualified contributors for the purpose of paying the higher education expenses of the account beneficiary, i.e., the student.

Contributions to an education IRA are nondeductible. The maximum amount that can be contributed each year to an education IRA is $500 (except in the case of rollover contributions). This amount will be phased out for contributors with modified adjusted gross income between $95,000 and $110,000 ($150,000 to $160,000 in the case of married couples filing jointly). Contributions may be made only in cash and cannot be made after the beneficiary reaches age 18.

> **Observation:** Although education IRAs operate in a manner similar to deductible IRAs established under present law, the $500 annual contribution amount operates independently from the limitations on other IRA contributions.

The new law also provides that funds from an education IRA are considered distributed to pay qualified education expenses if the funds are used to make contributions to or to purchase tuition credits from a qualified tuition program, as described above.

Amounts remaining in an education IRA must be distributed to the beneficiary before age 30. Earnings on such distributions will be included in income and subject to a 10-percent penalty if not used for education. However, tax-free and penalty-free transfers and rollovers are permited from one education IRA to another if the beneficiary is a family member.

The provisions governing contributions to and distributions from qualified tuition plans and education IRAs generally apply after December 31, 1997.

Student Loan Interest Deduction

The new law provides an above-the-line deduction for interest paid on a qualified education loan during the first 60 months in which interest payments are required. The dollar limitation on the deduction is $1,000 for 1998, $1,500 for 1999, $2,000 for 2000, and $2,500 for 2001 and thereafter. The provision is effective for interest payments due and paid after December 31, 1997, on any qualified loan. The maximum deduction amount is not indexed for inflation.

Qualifying loans generally will include any debt incurred to pay the higher education expenses of the individual, spouse or dependent at the time the debt was incurred.

Coopers & Lybrand L.L.P.

Observation: For existing loans, payments will be deductible to the extent that the 60-month period has not expired. A loan and any refinancing is treated as a single loan for purposes of the 60-month rule.

The deduction will phase out for those with modified adjusted gross income between $40,000 and $55,000 for individuals and between $60,000 and $75,000 for those filing joint returns. These amounts will be indexed for inflation for tax years beginning after 2002. Individuals who are claimed as a dependent are not eligible for the deduction.

IRA Withdrawals

The new law provides that the 10-percent early withdrawal tax will not apply to distributions from IRAs (including the new Roth IRAs (see page 21)) if used to pay qualified higher education expenses of the individual, spouse, child or grandchild. Qualified expenses include tuition, fees, books, supplies, equipment, and room and board. The exception to the 10-percent early withdrawal penalty will apply to distributions after December 31, 1997, for expenses paid after that date for education furnished in academic periods beginning after such date.

Employer-Provided Education Exclusion

The present law exclusion for up to $5,250 of employer-provided education assistance is extended to cover courses beginning before June 1, 2000. The exclusion is still not available for graduate-level education.

Other Education Incentives

The new law also includes the following education incentives:

❑ repeal of the limitation on qualified Section 501(c)(3) bonds other than hospital bonds;

❑ increase in the arbitrage rebate exception for governmental bonds used to finance education facilities;

❑ additional incentives for education zones;

❑ expanded income exclusion for cancellation of certain student loans.

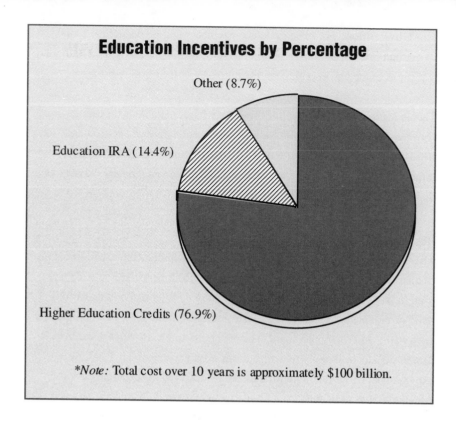

Education Incentives by Percentage

Other (8.7%)

Education IRA (14.4%)

Higher Education Credits (76.9%)

Note: Total cost over 10 years is approximately $100 billion.

Individual Retirement Accounts

To encourage individual savings, the new law expands the ability to make deductible contributions to individual retirement accounts, as well as creates new tax-favored accounts (so-called Roth IRAs) from which funds can be withdrawn without tax after a reasonable holding period for retirement or certain special purposes, such as first-time home ownership.

Deductible IRAs

The new law increases the adjusted gross income phaseout limits for deductible IRA contributions for an individual or spouse who is an active participant in an employer-sponsored retirement plan as follows:

Coopers & Lybrand L.L.P.

Deductible IRAs — Income Phaseout Limits

| Tax Years | Phaseout Range | |
	Single	Joint
1998	$30,000 – 40,000	$50,000 – 60,000
1999	31,000 – 41,000	51,000 – 61,000
2000	32,000 – 42,000	52,000 – 62,000
2001	33,000 – 43,000	53,000 – 63,000
2002	34,000 – 44,000	54,000 – 64,000
2003	40,000 – 50,000	60,000 – 70,000
2004	45,000 – 55,000	65,000 – 75,000
2005	50,000 – 60,000	70,000 – 80,000
2006	same	75,000 – 85,000
2007 and thereafter	same	80,000 – 100,000

Under the new law, married individuals may make deductible contributions to an IRA even if their spouses are active participants in an employer-sponsored plan. This benefit phases out beginning at adjusted gross income of $150,000 and ending at $160,000.

It also provides that the 10-percent early withdrawal tax will not apply to an IRA (including a Roth IRA described below) for up to $10,000 of first-time homebuyer expenses, for payments and distributions in tax years beginning after December 31, 1997, as well as education expenses. See page 21. Note, however, that a portion, if not all, of the distributions may be taxable (in contrast to the Roth IRA discussed below).

Observation: First-time homebuyer expenses must be used within 120 days of distribution for such costs as settlement, financing or closing costs of the residence of the individual, spouse, child or ancestor of the individual or spouse. The $10,000 limit is a cumulative life-time limit for each individual.

IRAs: Summary

Type	Description	Limitations
Traditional IRA	Tax-deferred retirement account; eligible for both deductible and nondeductible contributions.	• $2,000/$4,000 annual contribution limit (in aggregate with Roth IRA contribution); • Deductible in 1998 if income is less than $40,000 for single, $60,000 for married, $160,000 for noncovered spouse; • Subject to 10% penalty for nonqualified distributions.
Roth IRA	Tax-free accumulation retirement account; nondeductible contributions.	• $2,000/$4,000 annual contribution limit (in aggregate with traditional IRA contribution); • Nondeductible; • Contributable amount is phased out if income exceeds $110,000 for single, $160,000 for married; • Subject to 10% penalty for nonqualified distributions.
Education IRA	Tax-free accumulation for educational purposes.	• $500 annual contribution limit; • Nondeductible contribution phases out if income exceeds $110,000 for single, $160,000 for married; • Subject to 10% penalty for nonqualified distributions.

Coopers & Lybrand L.L.P.

Roth IRAs

The new law permits qualified individuals to make maximum annual contributions of the lesser of $2,000 (reduced by the deductible IRA contribution) or compensation for the year to so-called Roth IRAs. Although the contributions to Roth IRAs are not currently deductible, the amounts within the accounts can accumulate tax-free and qualified distributions will not be included in income. The available contribution limit for Roth IRAs phases out ratably for single individuals with adjusted gross income ranging from $95,000 to $110,000 and $150,000 to $160,000 for married, filing jointly.

Both a husband and a wife can contribute up to $2,000 provided that the combined compensation of the couple is at least equal to the total contributed amount. Contributions to Roth IRA accounts may be made even after an individual reaches age 70^1/2.

> **Observation:** Individuals may wish to consider shifting up to $4,000 a year (if married) into either a deductible IRA or a Roth IRA account. In addition, the advantages of tax-free build-up inside such accounts could make them valuable investment vehicles for children with earned income.

Qualified distributions from Roth IRA accounts are not includible in gross income, nor subject to the additional 10-percent tax on early withdrawals. Qualified distributions must be made (1) after five tax years from the first contribution, and (2) after the individual reaches age 59^1/2, at the death of the individual, because of disability or for a qualified special purpose. Special purpose distributions include first-time home purchase. Other distributions are includible in income to the extent attributable to earnings and are subject to the 10-percent early withdrawal tax unless an exception applies (withdrawal without penalty is permitted due to death, disability, excess medical expenses, the purchase of health insurance for an unemployed individual or education expenses, see page 17).

Qualified individuals (those who have adjusted gross income of less than $100,000) will be permitted to roll over contributions from present law deductible or nondeductible IRAs into Roth IRA accounts before January 1, 1999, without penalty. The amount that would be includible in income is taken into income ratably over four years beginning with the tax year of the conversion.

Observation: In cases where an IRA is converted into a Roth IRA, the five-year holding period begins with the tax year of the conversion. Conversions can be made in a variety of ways, including notification of the IRA trustee of the desire to change.

Individual Simplification Provisions

Standard Deduction for Dependents

In an effort to simplify income tax reporting for children under age 14, new statutory exemptions will be allowed in determining taxable income for tax years beginning after 1997. Under prior law the regular income tax exemption was the lesser of (1) the individual standard deduction or (2) the greater of $500 (indexed to $700 in 1998) or earned income.

The new law allows a child under the age of 14 to add $250 (indexed) to earned income in order to determine the amount available for their regular tax deduction.

> **Example:** A child with $600 of earned income in 1998 will be allowed a deduction of $850 ($600 + $250) because this amount is less than the standard deduction of $4,250 but greater than the "kiddie" exemption of $700.

A similar change has been made to increase the alternative minimum tax (AMT) exemption amount for children under age 14. Under prior law, the AMT exemption allowed was the lesser of the single AMT exemption of $33,750 or $1,400 plus earned income.

Observation: In most cases, for practical reasons, a child is not able to use the full AMT exemption.

The new law increases the AMT exemption amount for a child under age 14 to the lesser of $33,750 or the sum of the child's earned income plus $5,000. The $5,000 amount is indexed for inflation after 1998.

Observation: Both the change to the regular tax and AMT tax for purposes of determining the tax liability of children will result in a simplification in cases where the new amounts would prevent the child (or parent) from computing a "kiddie" tax.

Estimated Income Tax Threshold

In an attempt to reduce the number of individuals subject to estimated tax payment requirements and potential penalties, the new tax law increases the de minimis threshold for estimated tax from $500 to $1,000, effective for tax years beginning in 1998.

Other Provisions

Other provisions in the new law cover simplification for:

❑ methods for computing SECA tax for farmers and other businesses;

❑ treatment of certain reimbursed expenses of rural mail carriers.

Capital Gains and Investments

Capital Gains Rate Reduction

Under prior law, an individual's net capital gains for assets held more than one year were taxed at the lower of their marginal tax rate or 28 percent.

The new law reduces the maximum rate on net capital gains of an individual from 28 percent to 20 percent, but it increases the holding period for assets to more than 18 months. (Note: for sales after May 6, 1997, and before July 29, 1997, that satisfy a 12-month holding period, the 20 percent rate applies). Any net capital gain that is currently taxed at a 15-percent rate will be taxed at a 10-percent rate (if held for more than 18 months). These rates will apply for both regular and alternative minimum tax purposes, which means that there is no AMT adjustment for the new capital gains rates.

> **Observation:** The increase in the holding-period to qualify for the most beneficial long-term capital gain treatment was added to the new law during final negotiations.

The new law also provides, eventually, that capital gain property held for more than five years will be taxed at the reduced rate of 18 percent. The 18-percent rate will be available for property that meets the five-year holding requirement and is acquired after December 31, 2000 (and thus cannot benefit anyone until 2006). Individuals holding capital assets on January 1, 2001, can elect to mark-to-market such assets by recognizing gain (but not loss) on that

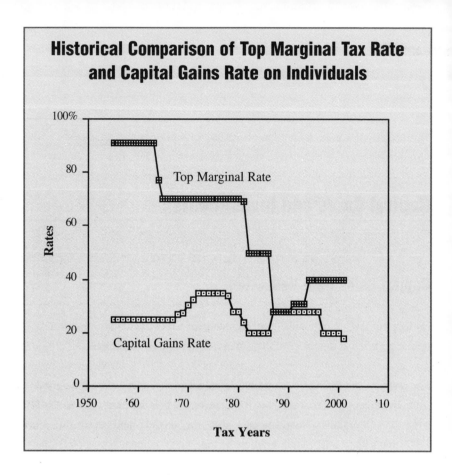

Historical Comparison of Top Marginal Tax Rate and Capital Gains Rate on Individuals

date. This will permit investors to treat the asset as if it was acquired on that date. The 10-percent rate for capital gains (for those in the 15-percent bracket) will be reduced to 8 percent for assets meeting the five-year holding period after December 31, 2000, regardless of the acquisition date.

> **Observation:** Recent sample data released by the IRS from Form 1040, Schedule D, indicates that almost 75 percent of all long-term gains reported holding periods of four years or less. Such transactions, however, represented less than 50 percent of the total value of total reported long-term gains.

The new law classifies capital assets that were held for a period of more than one year and less than 18 months as "mid-term gain" assets. Mid-term gain

Coopers & Lybrand L.L.P.

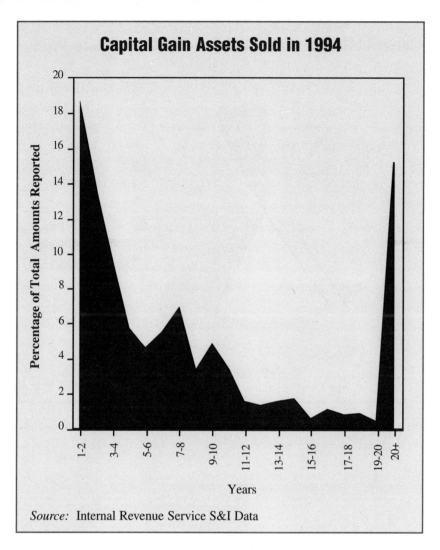

Capital Gain Assets Sold in 1994

Source: Internal Revenue Service S&I Data

assets will be subject to tax at a rate no higher than 28 percent. Collectibles are also subject to the 28 percent maximum rate (e.g., artwork).

Observation: There is an exception in the new law that provides that mid-term assets sold on or after May 7, 1997, and on or before July 28, 1997, would be eligible for the lower 20-percent maximum capital gains rate. This exception was added so that investors who had sold in reliance on the statements issued by the Chairmen of the Congressional tax-writing committees were not disadvantaged.

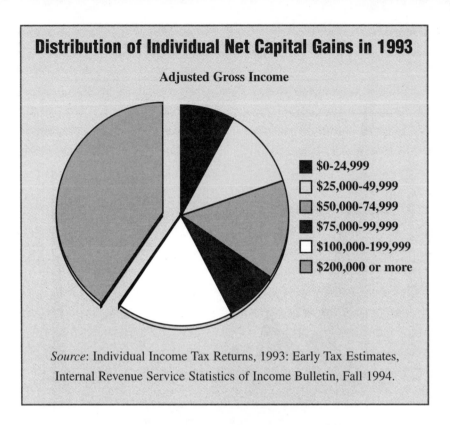

Distribution of Individual Net Capital Gains in 1993

Adjusted Gross Income

- $0-24,999
- $25,000-49,999
- $50,000-74,999
- $75,000-99,999
- $100,000-199,999
- $200,000 or more

Source: Individual Income Tax Returns, 1993: Early Tax Estimates, Internal Revenue Service Statistics of Income Bulletin, Fall 1994.

Observation: Provisions that would allow for indexing of certain capital assets and a reduced rate for corporate capital gains were not included in the new law. The indexing provision was especially nettlesome to the bipartisan budget negotiators and was dropped from the final version of the new law to avoid a potential Presidential veto.

Although the new law does not provide for any corporate capital gain rate reduction, corporations will be affected by the reduced individual rates in several ways. For example, corporations may be less inclined to increase dividend payouts, which would be taxed at higher marginal rates to shareholders, but will instead be inclined to maximize capital appreciation. Growth stocks and mutual funds generating returns in share price should be more attractive. Companies will also need to review the use of non-cash compensation in executive compensation programs. Incentive stock options will be more desirable because they can qualify for preferential capital gain treatment. In the case of

Coopers & Lybrand L.L.P.

restricted properties, there will be more of an incentive to freeze the compensation element through a Section 83(b) election.

> **Observation:** Investors will want to review their portfolios and capital gains strategies in light of the new lower rates and longer holding period requirements. Some investors will need to hold assets longer than in the past in order to qualify for the most preferential rate. Gifting strategies involving capital assets could also change.

> **Observation:** Now that capital gains are taxed even more favorably than ordinary income, the IRS may be more vigilant in applying Internal Revenue Code provisions that recharacterize capital gain income as ordinary income.

The Revenue Reconciliation Act of 1993 enacted targeted capital gains incentives for the sale of qualified small business stock held for more than five years. It provides for a 50 percent exclusion from gross income of gain for noncorporate shareholders so that the maximum capital gains rate on such stock is 14 percent. The new law does not change the capital gain treatment of qualified small business stock, and, therefore, such gains will remain taxed at no higher than 14 percent (28 percent rate x 50 percent exclusion), although the effective rate may be higher for individuals subject to AMT.

> **Observation:** The reduction in the top rate on capital gains to 20 and eventually 18 percent could reduce the attractiveness of the qualified small business stock. It is important to note, however, that the five-year holding period requirement enacted for such stock in 1993 is yet to be satisfied, that it remains to be seen how prevalent usage of this provision has been so far.

The new law also provides that the maximum tax rate on the gain from the sale or exchange of depreciable real property will be 25 percent for gain attributable to depreciation already claimed on the property (unrecaptured Section 1250 gain), with any remaining gain benefiting from the 20 percent and 18 percent maximum rates.

Example: An individual purchases a commercial office building for $1 million. After several years of depreciation, the adjusted basis is $700,000. If the building is sold for $1.2 million, the new law will tax the transaction as follows: $300,000 of recapture gain subject to recapture tax at no higher than 25 percent, $200,000 of gain in excess of original cost basis taxed at no higher than 20 percent (18 percent if held for 5 years starting after 2000).

Observation: Since unrecovered Section 1250 gain is taxed at a 25 percent rate, sellers of land and buildings will be more likely to attribute appreciation (and thus sales proceeds) to the land and away from the building in order to take advantage of the rate disparity. In contrast, a purchaser may be more inclined to allocate purchase price to a building due to the ability to claim depreciation deductions on the building.

Observation: Sellers of businesses will also benefit by allocating purchase price to goodwill, as opposed to covenants not to compete or various personal and real property, which may require ordinary income recapture. The ability to amortize goodwill (enacted in the Revenue Reconciliation Act of 1993) may make a purchaser of the business more amenable to such an allocation.

Observation: The ability to offset ordinary income with up to $3,000 of capital losses has not been modified by the new law.

The new provisions are applicable for assets sold or exchanged (and installment payments received) on or after May 7, 1997. Individuals receiving qualified installment payments from sales of assets in prior years will benefit from the new 20-percent rate.

Coopers & Lybrand L.L.P.

Capital Gains Summary

✔ Before May 7, 1997, the sale of an asset held for more than one year would be taxed at a maximum capital gains tax rate of 28 percent.

✔ For sales taking place between May 7, 1997, and July 28, 1997, the maximum capital gains tax rate on the sale of an asset held for more than one year is 20 percent.

✔ Effective for sales taking place after July 28, 1997, assets must be held for more than 18 months to qualify for the maximum 20 percent capital gains rate.

✔ Assets sold after July 28, 1997, that have been held for more than one year, but not more than 18 months, are now classified as "mid-term gains" subject to a maximum 28-percent capital gains tax rate.

Principal Residence Gain Exclusion

Prior law allowed for nonrecognition of gain on the sale of a principal residence, provided that the purchase price of the new principal residence was at least as much as the sales price of the old principal residence. In addition, taxpayers age 55 or older were granted a one-time exclusion of $125,000 of gain on the sale of a principal residence.

The new law permits an individual to exclude $250,000 ($500,000 if married filing jointly) of gain on the sale of a principal residence. In general the exclusion is allowed for each sale or exchange of a principal residence provided it had been treated as a principal residence for at least two of the preceding five years. If the two-year requirement is not met due to a change of employment, health or other unforeseen circumstance, the $250,000 ($500,000 if married filing jointly) exclusion is allowable based on a ratio of the qualifying months to 24 months.

In general, this provision is effective for sales of principal residences on or after May 7, 1997, and replaces the prior rollover and exclusion provisions. Alternate effective dates may be available in certain situations.

Principal Residence Exclusion

Filing Status	Personal Residence for 2 or more years: Exclusion	Personal Residence for less than 2 years:* Exclusion
Married, filing joint	$500,000	$\dfrac{\text{Qualifying months}}{24 \text{ months}} \times \$500,000$
Single	$250,000	$\dfrac{\text{Qualifying months}}{24 \text{ months}} \times \$250,000$

* Applicable in case of change of employment, health, or unforeseen circumstances.

Observation: The new $500,000 exclusion lowers the number of individuals paying capital gains tax on residences to roughly 10,000 per year from the current 150,000 per year and substantially simplifies the recordkeeping requirements for over 60 million households who own their own homes. However, individuals realizing gains in excess of the excludible amounts will no longer be able to benefit from the gain rollover accorded under prior law.

Observation: In addition to providing an exclusion for all individuals, regardless of age, the new law will be especially beneficial to those who have already taken advantage of the $125,000 one-time exclusion available under prior law. Individuals who would realize significant gains if they sold their principal residence under the new law may wish to reevaluate sales decisions as well as a variety of estate planning considerations.

Qualified Small Business Stock Gain Rollover

Under prior law, individuals were allowed to exclude 50 percent of the gain on the sale of "qualified small business stock." Half of the excluded gain was a minimum tax preference. Qualified small business stock in general must be held for at least five years and have been obtained in an original issuance from a corporation in an active trade or business, whose gross assets did not exceed $50 million at the time of issuance.

Effective after the date of enactment, the new law allows an individual to roll over the gain on the sale of qualified small business stock (if held for more than six months) if the proceeds are used to purchase other qualified small business stock within 60 days of the sale. In addition, the minimum tax preference amount has been reduced to 42 percent of the excluded gain.

Short-Against-the-Box and Similar Transactions

Under prior law, investors were often able to eliminate future risk of loss on certain appreciated financial positions (generally stocks, bonds, and partnership interests), while not recognizing any taxable income by entering into an offsetting position. These nonrecognition transactions allowed investors to remove cash from the transaction as if the appreciated position had been sold.

The new law requires that an investor recognize gain, but not loss, upon entering into a constructive sale of any appreciated position in stock, a partnership interest or certain debt instruments. A constructive sale is a transaction that, for all intents and purposes, is closed—i.e., the investor's risk of loss is gone—but for tax purposes, since the investor has not sold the instrument, the transaction is considered "open" and no tax triggering event has occurred. For instance, an investor enters into (1) a short sale, (2) an offsetting notional principal contract, or (3) a futures or forward contract with respect to the same or substantially identical property.

The gain on a constructive sale is determined by assuming that such position was sold, assigned or otherwise terminated at its fair market value on the date of the constructive sale and immediately repurchased.

Observation: Although the new law is aimed primarily at so-called "short-against-the-box" transactions, the provisions encompass other transactions designed to reduce or eliminate an investor's risk of loss, such as entering into a notional principal contract with respect to the same or substantially identical property. The short-against-the-box transaction is one where an investor borrows and sells shares identical to the shares the investor holds. By holding two precisely offsetting positions, the investor is insulated from economic fluctuations in the value of the stock. The short-against-the-box transaction allows the taxpayer to "borrow" a substantial portion of the value of the appreciated long stock without the risk that such stock will decline in value so that, economically, the transaction strongly resembles a sale of the long stock.

Observation: The new law does not address the treatment of options used to offset an appreciated position. This remains an area of concern for investors who will now need to await regulations from the Treasury.

The new law provides exceptions to the constructive sale rule for certain transactions. Appreciated financial positions that are marked-to-market and certain transactions that are closed within 30 days after the end of the tax year in which they are entered into would not fall within this provision.

The new law generally applies to constructive sales entered into after June 8, 1997. A transaction occurring before this date that would otherwise be treated as a constructive sale will not trigger gain recognition if the taxpayer identifies the offsetting positions of the earlier transaction within 30 days after the date of enactment.

Observation: Although the short-against-the-box rules are not investor favorable, the new law generally is not as detrimental as anticipated. The exception discussed above provides some relief for investors.

Mark-to-Market Accounting for Securities/Commodities Traders

The new law allows securities traders and commodity traders and dealers to elect mark-to-market accounting similar to that currently required for securities dealers.

Observation: The new law is not intended to apply to loans made to customers or receivables or debt instruments acquired from customers

Coopers & Lybrand L.L.P.

that are not received or acquired in connection with a trade or business as a securities trader.

Observation: Any adjustment necessary to make the change in accounting method for the tax year that includes the date of enactment is required to be taken into account ratably over a four-year period. For all other years, the adjustment will be governed by rules established by the Treasury.

Observation: For elections made for the first tax year ending after the date of enactment, the taxpayer must identify the securities or commodities to which the election will apply within 30 days of the date of enactment.

This election applies to tax years ending after the date of enactment.

Business

The new law cobbles together numerous provisions impacting businesses—both large and small. Some offer widespread benefits, including much-anticipated changes to the alternative minimum tax treatment of depreciable assets and extension of the research and experimentation credit. Others, such as the increased deduction for health insurance for self-employed individuals, are targeted at small business. The new law also includes changes in long-standing corporate rules that could negatively impact tax liability, such as the carryback and carryforward of net operating losses and general business credits. The following chapter explains the rules for the major corporate changes.

General Provisions

Net Operating Loss (NOL) and General Business Credit Carryback/Carryforward

Net Operating Losses

Under the prior law, net operating losses generally were required to be carried back 3 years and forward 15 years unless an election was made to forego the 3-year carryback. In certain situations, (e.g., "specified liability losses"), a 10-year carryback was permitted.

The new law limits the general NOL carryback period to 2 years and extends the NOL carryforward period to 20 years. This is a fundamental change to a long-standing benefit available to NOL taxpayers.

Under the new law, companies with NOLs will need to implement creative tax planning strategies to utilize NOLs within a shorter carryback period.

> **Example:** A taxpayer expecting to be in an NOL position for 1997 and 1998 with carryback potential in 1994 and 1995 should consider accelerating deductions or deferring income in 1997. By implementing such a strategy, the taxpayer will be able to increase its 1997 NOL and therefore its carryback to offset past income. resulting in a potential cash refund.

Observation: The effective date of this law change creates additional pressure in 1997 for corporate tax planning regarding the use of NOLs. Losses created in 1997 can be carried back to 1994; however, beginning in 1998, NOLs can be carried back only to 1996, reflecting the two-year drop-off once the law is enacted.

Specified liability losses (SLLs) can still be carried back 10 years under the new law. Thus, to the extent that companies have SLLs, there is an opportunity to avoid the impact of the shortening of the NOL carryback period.

Observation: The new law also does not apply to corporate capital losses, which retain a three-year carryback period, nor does the new law apply to NOLs arising from casualty losses of individuals or those incurred by farmers and small businesses in Presidentially declared disaster areas.

The new law is effective for NOLs for tax years beginning after the date of enactment.

General Business Credits

Under prior law, unused or limited business tax credits were carried back 3 years and then forward 15 years. The new law requires that unused business credits be carried back one year and forward 20 years. This change is effective for business tax credits arising in tax years beginning after December 31, 1997.

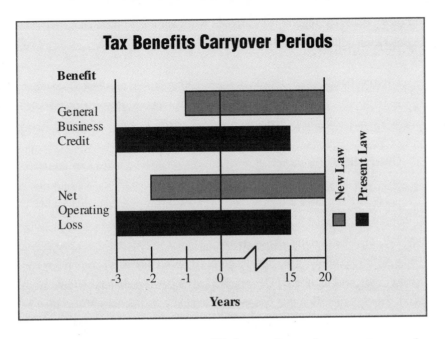

Tax Benefits Carryover Periods

Observation: To the extent qualified expenditures that generate general business credits can be accelerated into 1997, an additional two-year carryback benefit can be secured.

Example: If corporation Y had an unused business tax credit in 1998, Y would carry it back to 1997. To the extent that the 1998 unused tax credit is not absorbed in 1997, it would then be carried over to years 1999 through 2018.

Alternative Minimum Tax Provisions

Conform Depreciable Lives

The corporate AMT is highly complex and has proven to be a controversial tax. Efforts to repeal the corporate AMT outright failed with this tax legislation. In lieu of complete repeal, however, the new law conforms the recovery periods used for purposes of the AMT to those used for regular tax purposes for all taxpayers for property placed in service after December 31, 1998.

AMT depreciation continues to utilize the 150-percent declining balance method, with a switch to the straight-line method for tangible personal property. Therefore, taxpayers using the double declining balance method for these assets for regular tax purposes will continue to have an AMT depreciation adjustment.

> **Observation:** Assets placed in service after 1998 typically will continue to be subject to an AMT depreciation adjustment. Multiple depreciation schedules will still be required for these assets.

> **Observation:** The depreciation adjustment has pushed many capital-intensive companies into paying AMT. With a reduced depreciation adjustment going forward, these companies are much less likely to encounter the AMT.

AMT Repeal for Small Corporations

The new law completely repeals the corporate AMT for small corporations for tax years beginning after December 31, 1997. A "small corporation" is defined as a corporation that had average annual gross receipts of less than $5 million for the three-year period beginning after December 31, 1994. A corporation that meets the $5 million gross receipts test will continue to be treated as small business corporation exempt from the AMT provided its average annual gross receipts do not exceed $7.5 million. If a corporation fails to meet the $7.5 million gross receipts test, then it will become subject to corporate AMT, but only with respect to preferences and adjustments that relate to transactions and investments entered into after the corporation loses its status as a small business corporation.

Further, if a corporation does not have to pay the AMT because it is a small corporation, any allowable minimum tax credit carryovers from previous AMT tax years may not exceed the corporation's regular tax liability (reduced by other credits) over 25 percent of the corporation's regular tax (reduced by other credits) in excess of $25,000.

AMT and Installment Sales by Farmers

Under the current IRS ruling position, a cash-method farmer realizes income in the year farm commodities are sold, and is precluded from reporting income from deferred sales contracts under the installment method for AMT purposes.

Responding to Congressional pressure, the IRS declared that it would not enforce this position for tax years beginning before January 1, 1997. The new law statutorily overrules the IRS position and provides that, for purposes of the AMT, farmers may use the installment method of accounting.

Reporting of Taxable Income from Deferred Sales Contracts by Farmers		
	Regular Tax	**AMT**
Prior Law	As cash received	In first year of contract
New Law	As cash received	As cash received

The new law is retroactively effective for dispositions in tax years beginning after 1987.

Corporate-Owned Life Insurance

The new law makes dramatic changes to corporate- and business-owned life insurance. Included among these changes are provisions that reduce the benefits of life insurance to business purchasers by adding premium deduction limitations, interest deduction limitations and pro rata allocation of interest expense to policy cash values. All of these changes are effective for contracts issued after June 8, 1997.

Premium Deduction Limitation

Under prior law, no deduction was allowed for premiums paid on any life insurance policy covering the life of any officer or employee, or of any person financially interested in any trade or business carried on by the taxpayer, if the taxpayer is directly or indirectly a beneficiary under such policy.

The new law expands the limitation in two ways to clarify that no deduction will be allowed for premiums paid on any life insurance policy, or endowment or annuity contract, if the taxpayer is directly or indirectly a beneficiary under the policy or contract, even if the insured life is not an officer, employee or financially interested person.

Although the new law is ambiguous, it may eliminate the ability of mortgage lenders to deduct premiums paid on life insurance for business risks.

> **Observation:** For mortgage companies and banks, what does direct and indirect benefit mean? If a mortgage lender or bank could obtain repayment from the estate, but collects from the policy instead, the lender is no better off, but the estate is enriched by the amount of the coverage. Who is the beneficiary?

Interest Deduction Limitation

The new law also extends the prior law limitation on deducting interest on life insurance on officers and employees to now apply to coverage on all individuals. The law will eliminate the chance to deduct the interest when borrowing on a life insurance policy to invest the proceeds.

Prior law substantially limits the deductibility of interest on debt incurred to purchase or carry life insurance or annuity policies, or to purchase or carry tax-exempt obligations. In addition, in the case of a financial institution, a proration rule provides that no deduction is allowed for that portion of the taxpayer's interest that is allocable to tax-exempt interest. The new law expands this interest deduction disallowance by applying to new policies rules similar to the financial institution rules.

Prior law also provides that if a life insurance contract is sold ("transferred for value"), then the policy proceeds are taxable income except for the amount paid for the policy plus other amounts paid by the transferee after the transfer (effectively basis). Under the new law, "other amounts paid" will include interest paid by the transferee with respect to indebtedness on the contract if the interest is not deductible.

Disallowance of Interest on Debt to Fund Life Insurance

For a taxpayer other than a natural person, no deduction will be allowed for the portion of unrelated interest expense allocable to "unborrowed policy cash surrender values" with respect to any life insurance policy or annuity or endowment contract for which the business is directly or indirectly the beneficiary. Unrelated interest expense is allocable to the policy based on the ratio of the taxpayer's:

(1) average unborrowed policy cash values of life insurance policies, and annuity and endowment contracts, issued after June 8, 1997,

to

(2) average unborrowed policy cash values of life insurance policies, and annuity and endowment contracts (whether issued before or after June 8, 1997), plus the average bases for all other assets of the taxpayer.

In determining "unborrowed policy cash surrender values," life insurance policies and annuity and endowment contracts covering, at the time of issue, the life of a 20-percent owner, an active employee, officer or director of the taxpayer are not be taken into account. (A policy on a 20-percent owner may be a joint policy on the 20-percent owner and the owner's spouse.)

All members of a controlled group are considered one taxpayer for purposes of applying these rules. In the case of a partnership or S corporation, the new law would apply at the partnership or corporate level.

If interest expense is disallowed under other rules limiting interest deductions with respect to life insurance policies, endowment or annuity contracts, tax-exempt interest, then the disallowed interest expense is not taken into account under the new law, and the average adjusted bases of assets will be reduced by the amount of debt for which interest is so disallowed. The new law will be applied before present law rules relating to capitalization of certain expenses where the taxpayer produces property.

> **Observation:** Although it is unclear, the new law may provide no relief if an insurance policy is later surrendered with the inside build-up becoming taxable. Thus, the purchaser could potentially pay tax on the inside build-up twice: first through the new law's special allocation rule, and second on surrender of the policy.

The rules described above do not apply to life or property and casualty insurance companies. Instead, the "increase…in policy cash values" is treated as if it were tax-exempt interest or a dividend-received deduction. Thus, the policy holder share rules for life insurers and the proration rules for P&C companies will make significant portions of this amount taxable.

> **Observation:** The increase in policy cash values is defined to include cash values, commissions and asset management fees that would be imposed if the policy were surrendered. The effects of premiums paid and nontaxable distributions (such as loans) are not considered.

Contract Lapses Under Effective Date Provisions of the COLI Rule

Prior law provides for a phase in of the corporate-owned life insurance (COLI) rule denying interest deductions on policies with certain transition rules. The new law clarifies that, under the transition relief provided under the COLI rule, the 4-out-of-7 rule and the single premium rule of prior law are not to apply solely by reason of a lapse occurring October 13, 1995, by reason of no additional premiums being received under the contract .

The relief allowing insurers the deduction of deferred acquisition costs on transition policy surrenders has been repealed.

Welfare-to-Work Tax Credit

In an effort to shore up some of the cuts in welfare, and to give employers additional incentive to hire and retain welfare recipients, the new law offers a credit for qualified wages paid to long-term family assistance recipients. The provision defines "long-term family assistance recipients" as any individual who is certified by the designated local agency. A similar credit was enacted in 1996 under the term "work opportunity tax credit," which is in effect for targeted individuals hired after September 30, 1996, and before October 1, 1997 (now extended to June 30, 1998; see page 51).

> **Observation:** If an employer is allowed a credit for wages paid to a long-term family assistance recipient, the employee cannot also be treated as a member of a targeted group for purposes of the "work opportunity tax credit."

For the first year beginning on the date of hire, the new wage credit is 35 percent on the first $10,000 of wages in the first year of employment, and 50 percent of the first $10,000 wages in the second year.

The term "wages" has the same general meaning as provided under the 1996 work opportunity tax credit. It also includes amounts paid by the employer but excludible by the employee, such as health insurance premiums, contributions to accident and health plans, education assistance programs, and dependent care assistance programs.

Long-Term Family Assistance Recipients

Long-term family assistance recipients must be certified by the designated local agency, but could include members of a family that:

❑ has received family assistance for at least 18 consecutive months ending on the hiring date;

❑ has received family assistance for at least 18 months (whether or not consecutive) after the date of enactment of the credit if they are hired within 2 years after the date the 18-month total is reached; and

❑ is no longer eligible for family assistance because of either federal or state time limits, if hired within 2 years after the federal or state time limits made the family ineligible for family assistance.

This special tax credit will be granted to employers for new hires who begin work after December 31, 1997, but before May 1, 1999.

Enhanced Deduction for Corporate Contributions of Computer Technology

Gifts of computer technology and equipment, such as software and computer equipment, by C corporations qualifies for the augmented charitable deduction equal to its basis in the property plus one-half of the amount of ordinary income that would have been realized if the property had been sold, but no more than twice the basis of the property. Contributions must be made to elementary or secondary schools or private foundations that support elementary and secondary education. Gifts must be made no later than two years after the date the property was acquired by the corporation and is effective for contributions made in tax years beginning after 1997 and before January 1, 2000.

Observation: This provision is similar to C corporation deductions allowed for contributions of appreciated inventory to charities for related purposes.

Financial Products

Dividend-Received Deduction

Prior law provides corporations holding stock of another corporation with a dividend-received deduction (DRD). The amount of the deduction is based on the percentage (by vote and value) of payor stock owned by the recipient. Under prior law, the DRD was allowed only if the recipient corporation satisfied a 46-day holding period (91 days for certain dividends on preferred stock). This holding period was required to be satisfied only once, rather than prior to each dividend.

The new law provides that the DRD will be available only if the recipient holds the stock for more than 45 days during a 90-day period. The 90-day period begins 45 days before the ex-dividend date. It also requires that stock with a dividend preference be held for more than 90 days during an 180-day period beginning 90 days before the ex-dividend date.

The new law is generally effective for dividends paid or accrued after 30 days after the date of enactment with an exception for dividends received within two years of the date of enactment for certain stock held on June 8, 1997, and all times thereafter until the dividend is received.

> **Observation:** The provision is targeted at attempts to market dividend-paying stocks to corporate investors with accompanying attempts to hedge or relieve the holder from risk for most of the holding period, after the initial holding period is satisfied. Opponents of the provision argued that prior law rules are sufficient to prevent short-term investment for purposes of earning largely tax-free income because the investing corporation must hold the instrument at risk for at least one dividend period.

> **Observation:** Congressional taxwriters rejected the original Clinton Administration proposal to reduce the DRD to 50 percent or deny the DRD for preferred stock with certain non-stock characteristics.

Pooled Debt Obligations — Credit Card Receivables

The new law requires taxpayers holding a pool of debt obligations, such as credit card receivables, to accrue interest or original issue discount on such

Coopers & Lybrand L.L.P.

pool based on a reasonable assumption regarding the timing of the payments of the accounts in the pool.

> **Observation:** This new law provisions particularly impact the year-end income of companies with credit card operations. These companies are now required to make reasonable assumptions as to what portion of the balances will be paid off within the "grace period" and to accrue interest income through year-end for that portion. Companies then will need to adjust such accruals in the following year to reflect the extent to which such prepayment assumptions reflected actual payments received after year-end. Under the prior law, companies generally were not required to make such accruals.

> **Observation:** If a taxpayer is required to change its method of accounting under the new law, any adjustment would be included in income ratably over a four-year period.

> **Observation:** Regulations may exempt "small" retailers from the new law; however, "small" is not defined by the statute.

The new law is effective for tax years beginning after the law is enacted.

Interest Deductions on Certain Debt Instruments Disallowed

Whether an instrument qualifies for tax purposes as debt or equity is determined on the facts and circumstances of the particular instrument, based on principles developed in case law. Under the new law, no deduction is allowed for interest on an instrument issued by a corporation (or issued by a partnership to the extent of its corporate partners) that is payable in the stock of the issuer or a related party. This includes an instrument of which a substantial portion is mandatorily convertible or convertible at the issuer's option into stock of the issuer or a related party. However, it is not expected that the provision will apply to convertible debt if the conversion price is significantly higher than the market price of the stock on the issue date.

> **Observation:** Early in 1997, the Clinton Administration targeted several areas of the debt/equity classification debate proposing to deny interest deductions on long-term debt and products, such as monthly income pre-

ferred shares (MIPS), and deferring interest deductions on certain convertible debt—instruments referred to as liquid yield option notes (LYONs). In response to the Clinton Administration proposals, Congress chose to include restrictions only on targeted instruments that are payable in stock of the issuer.

Observation: The new law addresses only the deduction of interest for the issuer. Unlike distributions on preferred stock, a corporate holder would not qualify for the dividend-received deduction.

The provision is effective for instruments issued after June 8, 1997, but will not apply to an instrument (1) issued pursuant to a written agreement that is binding on such date and at all times thereafter, (2) described in a ruling request submitted to the IRS on or before such date, or (3) described in a public announcement or filing with the Securities and Exchange Commission on or before such date.

Gains and Losses from Certain Terminations with Respect to Property

The new law includes amendments to several provisions regarding gain/loss treatment:

❏ Gain/loss from the cancellation, lapse, expiration or other termination of a right or obligation with respect to all property that is a capital asset in the hands of the taxpayer is capital (previously, the law generally applied only to publicly traded property). Thus, the new law applies to interests in real property (i.e., amounts received to release a lessee from a requirement that the premises be restored on termination of the lease) and non-actively traded personal property (i.e., forfeiture of a down payment under a contract to purchase stock).

❏ The new law provides that, if a taxpayer enters into a short sale of property and the property becomes worthless, gain is recognized as if the transaction were closed, i.e., capital gain.

❏ The new law repeals a special exemption previously available for debt obligations issued by natural persons and terminates a special grandfather debt rule.

These provisions have varying effective dates.

Coopers & Lybrand L.L.P.

Small Business

Home Office Deduction

A person may be allowed a deduction for business expenses associated with the business use of a portion of their home. A deduction is allowed only with respect to the portion of the home that is used exclusively and regularly in one of three ways:

- ❑ the portion of the home is considered the principal place of business for a trade or business;
- ❑ it is used to meet with patients, clients or customers in the normal course of the taxpayer's trade or business; or
- ❑ the portion so used constitutes a separate structure not attached to the dwelling unit.

New Test for Home Office Deduction

Home office deduction for administrative or managerial activities of a trade or business.

- ❑ Is the home office used for administrative or managerial activities in connection with a trade or business?
- ❑ Is the home office used exclusively in connection with a trade or business?
- ❑ Are administrative or managerial activities not substantially performed at a different fixed location?

If the answer to all three questions is yes, the homeoffice deduction may be available.

For tax years beginning after December 31, 1998, the new law allows a home office to qualify for deductions under an expanded definition of a "principal place of business." The new definition includes areas exclusively used to conduct administrative or management activities of a trade or business if there is no other fixed location of the trade or business where the taxpayer conducts substantial administrative or management activities of the trade or business. Employees are allowed similar treatment only if such exclusive use is for the convenience of the employer.

> **Observation:** This rule will permit some individuals to conduct minimal paperwork at a fixed location of the business without jeopardizing the home office deduction. Additionally, services or meetings with customers, clients or patients may take place at a separate fixed business location.

> **Observation:** This provision will aid the growing number of individuals who manage their business activities from home and is responsive to the "information revolution." In addition, it allows more people business deductions when they work at home via the computer. Typical expenses that are deductible in connection with a home office deduction include a portion of rent, depreciation, repairs and a portion of utilities.

Health Insurance Deduction for Self-Employed Individuals

Self-employed individuals can deduct a portion of the amount paid for health insurance for themselves, a spouse and dependents, provided that the individual is not able to participate in an employer-subsidized health plan maintained by an employer of the individual or the individual's spouse. Under prior law, the deductible percentage was scheduled to increase from 40 percent in 1997 to 80 percent by 2006.

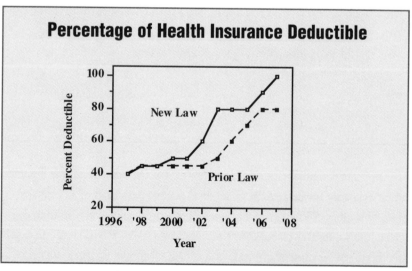

Coopers & Lybrand L.L.P.

The new law increases the deduction for self-employed health insurance up to 100 percent over several years. For tax years beginning in 1997, the deduction is 40 percent of health insurance expense, 45 percent in 1998 and 1999, 50 percent in 2000 and 2001, 60 percent in 2002, 80 percent in 2003 through 2005, 90 percent in 2006, and 100 percent in 2007 and thereafter.

Electronic Federal Tax Payment System

Congress, perceiving that employers needed more time to become familiar with the Electronic Federal Tax Payment System (EFTPS) arrangement of paying taxes, extended the deadline for compliance through June 30, 1998. The Treasury Department will not assess penalties for failure to use electronic payments until after this date. This leeway is granted only to businesses that were first required to begin EFTPS payments on or after July 1, 1997. See page 119.

Expiring Provisions

The new law extends several so-called "expiring provisions," which have expired or were scheduled to expire in 1997, including the research and

Extension of Expiring Provisions

| | | Date to which extended | | |
Provision	Date from which effective	6/30/98	5/31/00	Permanent
Research tax credit	June 1, 1997	●		
Contributions of appreciated stock to private foundations	June 1, 1997	●		
Work opportunity credit*	October 1, 1997	●		
Orphan drug credit	June 1, 1997			●
Employer-provided educational assistance	January 1, 1997		●	

* Credit Modified

experimentation credit (R&E credit), the deduction for contributions of qualified appreciated stock to private foundations, the work opportunity tax credit
(WOTC), the orphan drug credit, and the exclusion for employer-provided
undergraduate education.

Accounting Methods

Inventory Shrinkage

Retailers and wholesalers, and to a lesser extent manufacturers, need to take
shrinkage (e.g., bookkeeping errors, theft and breakage) into account in computing ending inventory. When physical inventories are not taken at year-end,
inventory shrinkage through year-end must be estimated by the taxpayer, or
not considered in computing taxable income until the following year.

For a number of years, the IRS has argued that, for tax purposes, estimated
shrinkage may not be taken into account in computing ending inventory. The
Tax Court in 1993, and again in 1997, rejected that position, but determined
that the methodology used to estimate the incurred shrinkage must be
reviewed to determine whether it results in a clear reflection of income.

For those taxpayers who do not take a physical inventory on the last day of
their tax year at all locations, Congress has decided to codify the Tax Court's
decision. The new law provides that a method of keeping inventories will not
fail to clearly reflect income solely because it includes an adjustment for the
shrinkage estimated to occur through the taxpayer's year-end if the taxpayer
performs a physical count of inventories:

❑   at each location;
❑   on a regular and consistent basis; and
❑   makes proper adjustments to its inventories and to its estimating methods
    to adjust from their estimates to the actual shrinkage incurred.

> **Observation:** Under the new law, taxpayers are permitted to change
> their method of accounting to utilize estimates of inventory shrinkage
> when physical inventories are taken at other than year-end, *assuming
> that their current method does not utilize estimates of inventory*

If companies typically take their physical inventories:	*...Then their associated inventory shrinkage is:*
• At all locations on the last day of their tax year	• Actual shrinkage is known through the year-end.
• At all locations on one date other than the last day of their tax year	• Shrinkage through year-end must either be estimated or not taken into account until the following year.
• At different locations at different times during their tax year (i.e., cycle counting)	• Shrinkage through year-end must either be estimated or not taken into account until the following year.

shrinkage. The Section 481(a) adjustment necessary to make the accounting method change is taken into taxable income pro-rata over a four-year spread.

The new law does not provide direct guidance for determining whether, in a particular fact situation, inventories that include adjustments for shrinkage result in a clear reflection of income. However, the Conferees did indicate that they expect the Treasury to issue guidance to establish one or more safe harbor methods to estimate shrinkage that will be deemed to result in a clear reflection of income, and to provide for an automatic election of a safe harbor method by taxpayers.

Observation: The Conference Report provides specific details regarding the expected features of safe harbor for retailers. These include such items as the definition of a historical ratio of shrinkage to sales to be determined for each store or each department, what to do in the case of a new store or department, and that a lookback adjustment would not be required.

The new law is effective for tax years ending after the date of enactment.

Exclusion of Retail Tenant Allowances

It is common practice for real estate landlords to provide cash allowances (or reductions in rent) to tenants that enter into leases. These allowances are meant to enable the tenant to improve or construct the premises, often in the form of an interior "buildout." With respect to retail industry store locations, the IRS position has been that, if the landlord does not own the improvement or construction, the tenant has income in the amount of the allowance. This position is set forth in a 1996 IRS Retail Industry Coordinated Issue paper.

The new law excludes from a tenant's income allowances received in cash (or treated as a rent reduction) from a landlord under a short-term lease of retail space, when the purpose of allowance is for the tenant's construction of, or improvement to, the leased premises. The exclusion applies only to the extent the allowance does not exceed the amount expended by the tenant on nonresidential real property.

The construction or improvement must be part of, or otherwise present at, retail space used by the tenant. Retail space means a location used by a lessee in its business of selling personal property or services to the general public. The construction or improvement must also revert to the landlord at the termination of the lease. A "short-term lease" is defined as a lease for the occupancy or use of retail space for a term of 15 years or less. In determining a lease term, renewal options other than those based on fair market value at the time of renewal are taken into account.

The new law also provides that the landlord will treat the amounts expended on the construction allowance as nonresidential real property, which is depreciated over a 39-year recovery period.

The new law authorizes regulations to be issued providing reporting requirements to ensure compliance by both landlords and tenants.

The provision applies to leases entered into after the date of enactment. The legislative history states that Congress intended no inference as to the treatment of allowances that are not subject to the provision.

Other Accounting Method Provisions

- ❏ tighten phaseout rules for cash-method family farms;
- ❏ simplify look-back rules for long-term contractors;
- ❏ provide deductions for Brownfields remediation;
- ❏ limit income forecast method to films, etc.;
- ❏ provide three-year MACRS life for certain rent-to-own property;
- ❏ eliminate installment method reporting for certain sales of personal property by a manufacturer to a dealer.

Miscellaneous Provisions

Extension of FUTA Excise Surtax

Under prior law, a temporary surtax of 0.2 percent of taxable wages was added to the permanent 0.6-percent FUTA tax rate. This temporary FUTA surtax was scheduled to expire on December 31, 1998.

The new law extends the temporary surtax rate through December 31, 2007. It also increases the limit from 0.25 percent to 0.5 percent of covered wages on the Federal Unemployment Account in the Unemployment Trust Fund.

> **Observation:** This extension of the FUTA surtax is estimated to raise $6.4 billion over five years, making it the new law's second largest single source of revenue (after the extension and modifications of the Airport Trust Fund excise taxes).

Tax-Free Employee Parking or Taxable Cash Compensation

Under prior law, up to $165 per month of employer-provided parking is excludible from gross income. For the exclusion to apply, the parking must be provided in addition to, and not in lieu of, any compensation that is otherwise payable to the employee.

The new law provides that no amount is includible in the income of an employee merely because the employer offers the employee a choice between cash and employer-provided parking, effective for tax years beginning after December 31, 1997. The amount of cash offered is includible in income only if the employee chooses the cash instead of parking.

Oklahoma Indian Reservation Technical Correction

Under prior law, certain Indian reservation lands are eligible for Indian wage credits and development incentives (including accelerated depreciation for certain properties), effective January 1, 1994. The Omnibus Budget Reconciliation Act of 1993 defined "former Indian reservations in Oklahoma" in a way that covered the entire state of Oklahoma, once an Indian territory.

The new law provides a technical correction to clarify the definition of "former Indian reservations in Oklahoma" as including only lands that are within the jurisdictional area of an Oklahoma Indian tribe and are recognized as eligible for "Indian trust land status." The technical correction is retroactive to January 1, 1994, but transition relief is provided with respect to a return filed before March 18, 1997, but only if such return is the first return filed for the tax year in which the property was placed in service. The same transition relief is available with respect to wages for which benefits were claimed.

Involuntarily Converted Property and Related Persons

Generally, gain realized by a taxpayer from certain involuntary conversions of property is deferred to the extent the taxpayer purchases property similar or related in service or use to the converted property within a specified replacement period of time. Under the prior law, C corporations and certain partnerships with corporate partners generally were not entitled to defer gain by purchasing replacement property if the replacement property or stock was purchased from a related person.

Under the new law, the denial of deferral is expanded to any other taxpayer—including an individual—that acquires the replacement property from a related party unless the taxpayer has aggregate realized gain of $100,000 or less for the tax year with respect to converted property with aggregate realized gains.

The new law is effective for involuntary conversions occurring after June 8, 1997.

Coopers & Lybrand L.L.P.

Tax-Exempt Bonds

Currently, if gross proceeds from a governmental bond are spent within six months of its issuance, any arbitrage profits earned during that period from investments unrelated to the governmental purpose need not be rebated to the federal government. This spending requirement is deemed satisfied if all but the lesser of 5 percent of the gross proceeds or $100,000 is spent within the six-month period and the remainder is spent within one year.

The new law repeals the $100,000 limitation. The rebate requirement no longer applies to the earnings from bond proceeds related to certain types of construction issues to the extent that they are invested in a bona fide debt service fund. The availability of this exception, however, is conditioned upon satisfaction of the prior law 24-month spending requirements for the construction proceeds.

Prior law limits the amount of private activity bond proceeds (not including those from qualified Section 501(c)(3) bonds) that can be invested at a yield materially higher than the bond yield itself to 150 percent of the amount of the debt service for the bond year. Failure to comply with this restriction could have resulted in a violation of the overall arbitrage rules applicable to tax-exempt bonds.

The new law repeals the 150-percent debt service-based limitation. All arbitrage profits, however, earned on investments unrelated to the governmental purpose of the borrowing must be rebated to the federal government, including all earnings in excess of the bond yield derived from the investment of bond proceeds and subsequent earnings on such earnings.

All of these changes apply to bonds issued after the date of enactment.

District of Columbia Tax Incentives

The new law contains a series of targeted provisions designed to generate economic activity in the District of Columbia (D.C.). They include a zero capital gains rate on certain property and a tax credit for first-time homebuyers.

Mergers and Acquisitions

Tax-Free Spin-Offs — The "Morris Trust" Legislation

Morris Trust Repeal

Under prior law, a corporation could distribute the stock of a controlled corporation (Controlled) in a tax-free spin-off even if the distributing corporation (Distributing) was acquired immediately after the spin-off in a tax-free reorganization (a "Morris Trust" transaction). A prearranged tax-free acquisition of Controlled, on the other hand, would generally result in a failed tax-free spin-off if the Distributing shareholders failed to retain an interest in at least 80 percent of Controlled.

Several well-publicized transactions have been accused of exploiting the Morris Trust transaction by causing the acquired corporation to incur substantial debt prior to the spin-off, while transferring the proceeds to the other corporation. For example, Distributing would incur substantial debt and contribute the loan proceeds to Controlled prior to a spin-off (see diagram page 60). After the spin-off, Distributing would merge into a third-party corporation (Acquiror), in which Distributing shareholders would acquire a relatively small percentage of Acquiror's stock. Acquiror's assumption of Distributing's debt in the merger generally would be nontaxable to Distributing. This transaction was perceived by lawmakers to involve an effective "sale" of Distributing's assets for cash to Acquiror.

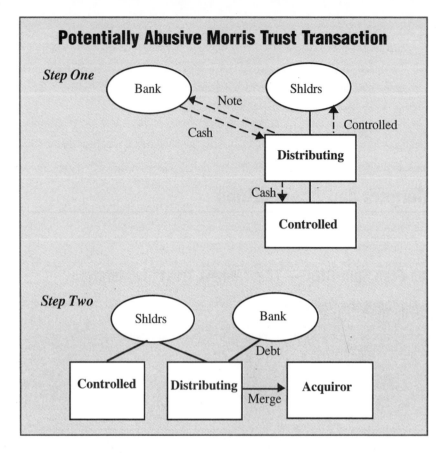

Potentially Abusive Morris Trust Transaction

Step One

Bank — Note — Shldrs

Cash

Controlled

Distributing

Cash

Controlled

Step Two

Shldrs — Bank

Debt

Controlled — **Distributing** — Merge → **Acquiror**

To prevent the perceived abuse (as well as to minimize differences between acquisitions of Distributing and acquisitions of Controlled), the new law taxes Distributing on a spin-off if, pursuant to a plan, 50 percent or more of the stock of either Distributing or Controlled (measured by voting power or value) is acquired by one or more persons. Acquisitions for this purpose may include a public offering.

The statute creates a presumption that there was a prohibited plan in place at the time of the spin-off if Distributing or Controlled is acquired within two years before or after the spin-off. Taxpayers may rebut this presumption by showing that the acquisition is unrelated to the spin-off.

Observation: In addition to reaching the potentially abusive Morris Trust transactions involving leveraging, the new law also affects non-

Coopers & Lybrand L.L.P.

leveraged Morris Trust transactions where companies merely wish to spin off an unwanted business prior to being acquired by a relatively larger company. It should be noted that only Distributing is taxed under the new law—the Distributing shareholders still receive Controlled stock tax-free if the spin-off otherwise qualifies for tax-free treatment.

The new law is generally effective for distributions after April 16, 1997, unless the transition rule applies. The transition rule provides that these changes will not apply if the acquisition is:

- ❏ made pursuant to an agreement binding on April 16, 1997;
- ❏ described in an IRS ruling request submitted by April 16, 1997; or
- ❏ described in an SEC filing or a public announcement by April 16, 1997.

Modified Definition of "Control"

Prior law required that the shareholders receiving Controlled stock have an interest in 80 percent of voting power and 80 percent of each class of non-voting stock after the distribution. The new law requires generally that shareholders receiving Controlled stock have an interest in more than 50 percent of voting power and value of the stock after the distribution.

> **Observation:** This provision effectively increases the amount of Controlled stock that may be offered in a public offering following a spin-off of Controlled from 20 percent to 49.9 percent. This modified definition of "control" also more clearly reflects the economic ownership of Controlled than the prior definition.

This modified definition of control is effective for transfers after the date of enactment, subject to similar transition rules.

Special Rule for Intragroup Spinoffs

The new law also makes Section 355 inapplicable to a spin-off within an affiliated group if it is part of an overall Morris Trust transaction subject to the new law. This means that intragroup spin-offs that precede an otherwise straightforward spin-off outside the group will continue to qualify as tax-free distributions.

Observation: In general, a principal effect of eliminating Section 355 for an intragroup spinoff that is part of a prohibited Morris Trust transaction will be to trigger into income any excess loss account that may exist for the distributed subsidiary, since the acquisition of Distributing or Controlled will cause the spin-off outside the group to be taxable in any event.

Observation: The lawmakers expressed several concerns relating to basis adjustments in the case of intragroup spin-offs, and authorized the Treasury to issue any regulations necessary to address these concerns.

This provision has the same effective date as the Morris Trust provisions above, except that, in general, the Treasury regulations regarding basis adjustments will be effective prospectively.

Certain Preferred Stock Treated as "Boot"

Prior law permitted preferred stock to be received tax-free in a Section 351 transaction, a corporate reorganization or a spin-off. However, debt received in exchange for stock in these transactions is taxable as "boot." Lawmakers were concerned that certain preferred stock instruments were relatively secure instruments that resembled debt and, accordingly, should not be eligible for nonrecognition. The new law treats "nonqualified preferred stock" received in various nonrecognition transactions as taxable boot.

Preferred stock is stock that is limited and preferred as to dividends and does not participate in corporate growth to any significant extent. Nonqualified preferred stock is preferred stock where, at the time of issuance, any of the following apply:

1) the shareholder has the right to require the issuer to redeem the stock;
2) the issuer is required to redeem the stock;
3) the issuer has the right to redeem the stock and it is more likely than not that such right will be exercised; or
4) the dividend rate on the stock varies with reference to interest rates, commodity prices or other similar indices.

Items 1, 2 and 3 apply only if the right or obligation may be exercised within 20 years of issuance and is not subject to a contingency that renders the likelihood of redemption or purchase remote. A right or obligation is disregarded for purposes of items 1, 2 and 3 if (i) no publicly traded corporations are involved and exercise can occur only upon the holder's death, disability or mental incompetency, or (ii) stock is received as compensation and the right or obligation may be exercised only upon separation from service.

The following exchanges are excluded from this gain recognition:

❏ certain exchanges of preferred stock for comparable preferred stock of the same or lesser value;
❏ an exchange of preferred stock for common stock;
❏ certain exchanges of debt securities for preferred stock of the same or lesser value; and
❏ exchanges of stock in certain recapitalizations of "family-owned corporations."

The new law applies to transactions after June 8, 1997, unless the transaction is:

❏ made pursuant to a written agreement binding on June 8, 1997;
❏ described in an IRS ruling request submitted by June 8, 1997; or
❏ described in an SEC filing or a public announcement by June 8, 1997.

> **Observation:** Preferred stock that effectively participates in corporate growth through a conversion privilege (e.g., a conversion into common stock) does not necessarily avoid "boot" classification under the new law. Such stock must be tested under the definition of preferred stock without regard to the conversion privilege.

Extraordinary Dividends

Under prior law, corporate shareholders receiving "extraordinary dividends" reduced the basis of their stock (but not below zero) by the portion of the dividends not taxed as a result of the dividends-received deduction. The excess nontaxed portion was not taxed as a gain until a later sale of the stock. Under the new law, a corporate shareholder must recognize gain immediately whenever the nontaxed portion of the extraordinary dividend exceeds the basis of the shareholder's stock. Thus, the gain is no longer deferred.

The new law also treats as an extraordinary dividend any redemption that is treated as a dividend due to options being counted as stock ownership, except as provided in regulations. Distributions in redemption of stock are treated as a dividend, rather than as a sale of the stock, if they do not result in a "meaningful reduction" in the shareholder's proportionate interest in the distributing corporation and if the redemption fails to meet several specific tests (e.g., a substantial reduction computation and a termination test). The determination of whether a redemption is treated as a dividend is made with reference to certain option attribution rules.

The new law curtails the ability of corporate shareholders to characterize certain redemptions as dividend distributions solely because of options held by such shareholders, by including in income the excess of the nontaxed portion of a dividend over the basis of the stock redeemed.

Reorganizations or other exchanges involving amounts that are treated as dividends under the "boot" provisions may be subject to the extraordinary dividend rules if, for example, the amount is treated as a dividend solely because of options held by the corporate shareholder.

In general, unless the distribution was made pursuant to a binding contract in effect on May 3, 1995, or a tender offer outstanding on May 3, 1995, the effective date of this provision is retroactive to distributions after May 3, 1995. An effective date of September 13, 1995, is substituted in certain cases.

> **Observation:** This legislation is in response to media attention regarding Seagram's use of the option provisions of the constructive ownership rules to largely "cash-in" its investment in DuPont while using the dividends-received deduction to shelter a large portion of the income from tax.

Sales of Stock to Related Corporations

A taxpayer's sale of stock of a controlled corporation to another controlled corporation is often treated for tax purposes as a dividend paid by the purchasing corporation. While individual shareholders generally prefer capital gains over dividends, corporate shareholders may prefer dividends because of the dividends-received deduction. If the corporate shareholder is not required to reduce the basis of its stock for the untaxed dividends, an inappropriate shifting of basis can result.

The Senate explanation provides the following example, illustrated in the diagram below. Assume that a domestic corporation (Controlling) owns 70 percent of the shares of a domestic corporation (Transferor) and all the shares of another domestic corporation (Acquiror). Transferor owns all of the 100 shares of a domestic subsidiary (Target) with a basis of $100. Acquiror has substantial earnings and profits. Transferor sells all but one of its Target shares to Acquiror for $99, their fair market value. Under prior law, the $99 payment is treated as a dividend to Transferor. Although Transferor received $99 from Acquiror for its other shares of Target and has not paid full tax on that receipt due to the dividends-received deduction, Transferor could claim

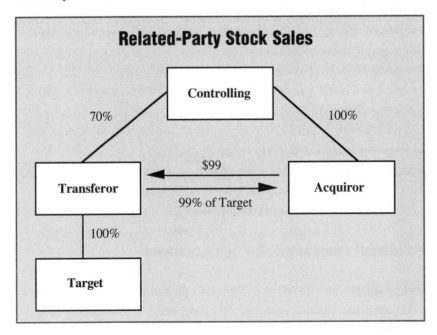

under prior law that the retained share of Target stock (worth $1) keeps its original basis of $100.

Under the new law, Transferor and Acquiror are treated as if (1) the Transferor transferred the Target stock to Acquiror in exchange for Acquiror stock in a Section 351 transaction, and (2) Acquiror immediately redeemed Acquiror's stock.

> **Observation:** In conjunction with changes to the "extraordinary dividend" provisions, the effect of the new law is to force a reduction in the basis of the retained Target stock (i.e., the $100 basis is reduced by the $99 payment), and to require immediate gain recognition whenever the payment exceeds the basis of such stock. This prevents Transferor from excluding income with the dividends-received deduction and subsequently incurring a loss on the sale of the remaining share of Target stock.

In the international setting, a foreign-owned U.S. corporation may attempt to claim foreign tax credits on deemed dividends received from a sale of a subsidiary to a commonly controlled foreign corporation, even though no foreign tax credits would flow to the U.S. seller if the purchasing corporation actually paid dividends to its foreign parent. The new law limits the foreign tax credit to situations where the selling shareholders would have been entitled to claim such credits if an actual distribution were made.

This provision is effective for distributions or acquisitions after June 8, 1997, except where there is:

- ❑ a written agreement binding on such date;
- ❑ a ruling request submitted to the IRS by such date; or
- ❑ a description in a public announcement or filing with the Securities and Exchange Commission on or before such date.

Investment Company Definition Expanded

Existing law provides that property transfers to investment companies do not qualify for nonrecognition treatment if the contribution results in diversification of the transferor's assets. A corporation or partnership (i.e., that is not otherwise a regulated investment company or real estate investment trust) is considered an investment company if more than 80 percent of its assets consist of certain enumerated investment assets (the Eighty Percent Test).

The new law was enacted to address concerns that prior law did not sufficiently prevent shareholders and partners from diversifying their investment assets through a nonrecognition transaction. Prior law counted readily marketable stocks and securities and interests in regulated investment companies (RICs) or real estate investment trusts (REITs) in the Eighty Percent Test. The new law expands the definition of investment assets that must be considered for purposes of the Eighty Percent Test to include, among others, the following:

❑ money;
❑ options, forward, and futures contracts;
❑ notional principal contracts and derivatives;
❑ foreign currency;
❑ interests in a publicly traded partnership;
❑ other entities holding (or convertible into) the foregoing assets; and
❑ certain interests in precious metals.

The new law applies to all transfers after June 8, 1997, in tax years ending after such date. There is an exception for written binding contracts in effect on June 8, 1997.

Estates, Gifts and Trusts

Unified Estate and Gift Tax Credit

Under prior law, each individual was entitled to make a combination of lifetime gifts and testamentary transfers of up to $600,000 in value without paying gift or estate tax. This amount was set in 1987 and has never been increased or adjusted for inflation.

The new law phases in an increased unified credit equivalent amount (now known as the applicable exclusion amount) from $600,000 to $1,000,000 by the year 2006.

Increased Unified Estate or Gift Exemption	
Year	**Exemption Amount**
1998	$625,000
1999	650,000
2000	675,000
2001	675,000
2002	700,000
2003	700,000
2004	850,000
2005	950,000
2006	1,000,000

> **Observation:** Had the $600,000 unified exemption amount been adjusted for inflation annually since its inception (based on an average of the monthly consumer price index), it would exceed $825,000 in 1997.

The unified exemption amount is supplemented by a special benefit made available to family-owned businesses. In addition, if more than 50 percent of an estate's value consists of a family-owned business interest, the first $1.3 million in value of the family-owned business may be excluded in calculating the value of the estate. A family-owned business interest must be an interest in a business in the United States. The business is considered family-owned if it is owned at least 50 percent by one family, 70 percent by two families or 90 percent by three families, so long as the decedent's family owns at least 30 percent of the business. In addition, there must be material participation for five of the eight years preceding the decedent's death by the decedent and/or a member of the decedent's family. The business must pass to a family member of the decedent, or an employee of the business. An additional estate tax may apply if such family members or employees fail to materially participate in the business within 10 years after the decedent's death.

This change is effective for decedents dying and gifts made after December 31, 1997.

> **Observation:** The family-owned business interest exclusion augments the applicable exclusion amount so that qualifying estates with family owned businesses will be able to exclude $1.3 million of value from estate taxation. With proper estate planning, a married couple can qualify to exclude $2.6 million of value of a family-owned business from taxation. The family-owned business benefit will be phased down to $300,000 upon reaching the year 2006 when the applicable exclusion amount reaches $1 million.

Coopers & Lybrand L.L.P.

> **Example:** Individual A passes away in 1998 with $3 million of land held for investment. Assuming no prior usage of the unified credit, $2.375 million will be subject to estate taxes (using a $625,000 applicable exclusion amount). Individual B also passes away in 1998. Individual B owned 100% of a business with a value of $1.6 million and land with a value of $1.4 million. Since the value of the business is more than 50% of the estate's value, the estate may exclude $1.3 million (an additional $675,000 over the exemption amount) of the value of the business, and thus the estate will be taxable on $1.7 million of value.

Installment Payment of Estate Taxes Attributable to Closely Held Businesses

To alleviate the liquidity problems of estates comprised of closely held businesses, prior law permitted qualifying estates to pay the estate tax over a maximum 14-year installment period. Interest on the tax incurred on the first $1,000,000 in value of the closely held business tax was imposed at a reduced rate of 4 percent. Principal payments were not required under the installment plan until year five.

The new law reduces the interest rate on the first $1,000,000 of the taxable portion of the estate comprised of the closely held business from 4 percent to 2 percent, and the interest on the remainder of the estate tax attributable to closely held businesses is reduced to 45 percent of the applicable rate for underpayment of tax. The reduced interest payments will no longer be deductible on estate or income tax returns.

The new provision is effective for decedents dying after December 31, 1997. Executors of estates of decedents dying prior to January 1, 1998, may elect to be subject to the new law.

Installment Payment of Estate Taxes Attributable to Closely Held Business — A Comparison

Prior Law	New Law
$600,000 unified exclusion amount	Applicable exclusion amount phased in over 9 years to $1,000,000.
4% interest rate on first $1 million taxable value	2% interest rate on first $1 million of taxable value
Statutory rate of interest on balance of payments	45% of statutory rate of interest on balance of payments
Interest payments deductible on estate return	Interest payments not deductible on estate return

Indexing of Other Estate and Gift Tax Provisions

Effective for decedents dying and gifts made after December 31, 1998, the new law indexes for inflation the following estate and gift tax limitations:

- ❏ $10,000 annual exclusion for gifts;
- ❏ $750,000 ceiling of special use valuation;
- ❏ $1,000,000 generation skipping transfer tax exemption;
- ❏ $1,000,000 value of closely held business receiving special interest treatment.

Charitable Remainder Trusts

In general, a charitable deduction is disallowed for a transfer of property to a charity if the donor retains an interest in such property. One exception to this rule is provided for remainder interests in charitable remainder annuity trusts

Coopers & Lybrand L.L.P.

(CRAT) or unitrusts (CRUT). A CRAT provides for a fixed annuity to a non-charity of at least 5 percent of the initial value of the contribution for the life of an individual or a term of less than 20 years. The remainder then passes to the charity. A CRUT is similar except the annual percentage payout is based on the value of the assets redetermined annually.

The new law prevents a trust from obtaining charitable remainder trust treatment if the annual payout percentage exceeds 50 percent.

In addition, the remainder interest which passes to the charity at the end of the term must be at least 10 percent of the initial value of assets contributed to the trust.

The new law also provides for the granting of relief to trusts which fail to meet the 10-percent requirement provided certain reformations are timely made.

In general, the new law applies to transfers to trusts made after July 28, 1997.

> **Observation:** The new 50-percent cap on annuity and unitrust payments was added in response to perceived abuses whereby some taxpayers were retaining annuity or unitrust payments in excess of 80 percent of the value of the trust. The new 10-percent floor on charitable interests will interact with the minimum 5-percent annuity or untitrust payment requirement so as to preclude certain taxpayers from creating charitable remainder trusts. For example, a 45 year-old father can no longer establish a charitable remainder unitrust which lasts for his lifetime and then the lifetime of his 21 year-old daughter because even if they retain the minimum 5-percent unitrust interest, the charitable remainder will be less than 10 percent (assuming the most recent federal interest rate).

Filing Requirements for Gifts to Charities

Under prior law, individuals who make gifts in excess of $10,000 to any one donee during the calendar year generally are required to file a gift tax return. This filing requirement applies to all gifts, whether charitable or non-charitable, and whether or not the gift qualifies for a gift tax charitable deduction.

Under the new law, gifts to charity are not subject to the gift tax filing requirements provided the entire value of the transferred property qualifies for the gift tax charitable deduction. The filing requirements for gifts of partial interests in property, however, would remain unchanged.

This change is effective for gifts made after the date of enactment.

Generation Skipping Taxes — Predeceased Parent Exception

The generation skipping tax applies to certain transfers that skip a generation. Such transfers include direct skips, taxable terminations and taxable distributions. Under prior law, a transfer from a grandparent to a grandchild where the intervening child/parent was deceased would not incur generation skipping tax as a direct skip, but a transfer from a trust funded by the grandparent to such a grandchild could incur generation skipping tax as a taxable termination or a taxable distribution. Also under prior law, a transfer from a grandparent to the grandparent's great-niece or great-nephew would be subject to generation skipping tax as a direct skip, even if the great-niece's or great-nephew's parent was not living at the time of the transfer.

Under new law, taxable terminations and taxable distributions can also take advantage of the predeceased parent exception, so that no generation skipping tax may be due. In addition, the predeceased parent exception will extend to transfers to collateral heirs if at the time of the transfer, the transferor has no lineal descendants.

The new law is effective for transfers, terminations and distributions after December 31, 1997.

Revocable Trusts

Estates and post-death revocable trusts (i.e., trusts that are revocable during decedent's lifetime and that become irrevocable upon decedent's death) are accorded different treatment for federal income tax purposes. For example, charitable deductions made by post-death revocable trusts are deductible only to the extent paid to charities, while an estate may take a deduction to the extent an amount has been permanently set aside for a charity (but not yet actually paid).

The new law provides for an election to treat certain post-death revocable trusts as part of an estate for a limited time in order to take advantage of the more beneficial Federal tax treatment accorded estates. The election must be made by the filing date of the estate's first income tax return, and is irrevocable once made.

> **Observation:** Revocable trusts are a popular "will substitute" for a variety of non-tax reasons, including the avoidance of probate. The new law, which helps to bridge the gap between the more-favored tax treatment of estates and that of trusts, may serve to increase the popularity of revocable trusts.

The new provisions are effective for estates of decedents dying after the date of enactment.

Distributions During First 65 Days of Estate's Tax Year

In general, income received by a trust or estate that is distributed to a beneficiary in the trust or estate's tax year "ending with or within" the tax year of the beneficiary is taxable to the beneficiary in that year; income that is retained by the trust or estate is initially taxable to the trust or estate.

Complex trusts, but not estates, can elect to have certain distributions made in the first 65 days following the end of the trust's tax year treated as having been made on the last day of that previous tax year.

The new law extends application of the 65-day rule to distributions by estates in order to prevent mismatching of income. Thus, an executor could elect to treat distributions paid within 65 days after the close of the estate's taxable year as having been paid on the last day of such taxable year.

This change is effective for tax years beginning after the date of enactment.

Separate Share Rules Applicable to Estates

In determining the amount of distributable net income of a trust that is allocable to its beneficiaries, substantially independent and separately administered shares of a single trust are treated as separate trusts for their respective beneficiaries. Consequently, activity such as accumulations or distributions in one separate share will not affect application of the tax rules or the tax consequences of activity in other shares, regardless of how many beneficiaries there are of any separate share or whether separate books of account are maintained for the separate shares. Under prior law, the separate share rule applied only to trusts; it had no application to estates.

The new law extends the application of the separate share rule to estates, effective for estates of decedents dying after the date of enactment.

Estate Executor and Beneficiaries Treated as Related Persons

Under the new law, an estate and a beneficiary of that estate will be treated as related persons for purposes of certain loss disallowance and recharacterization rules, except in the case of a sale or exchange in satisfaction of a pecuniary bequest.

This change is effective for tax years beginning after the date of enactment.

Waiver of Certain Rights of Recovery

Generally, transfers of terminable interests (such as life estates or annuities) do not qualify for the marital deduction. However, there is a major exception to the terminable interest rule for "qualified terminable interest property" (QTIP). QTIP is property passing from the decedent to a spouse who is entitled to all income from the property (or a portion thereof) for life, payable at least annually.

QTIP generally is included in the surviving spouse's gross estate upon his or her death. The surviving spouse's estate is entitled to recover the portion of the estate tax attributable to inclusion of QTIP from the person receiving the property, unless

Coopers & Lybrand L.L.P.

the spouse directs otherwise by will. Under prior law, a will provision specifying that all taxes shall be paid by the estate is sufficient to waive the right of recovery.

The new law provides that the right of recovery with respect to QTIP is waived only to the extent that language in the decedent's will (or revocable trust) specifically so indicates (e.g., by specific reference to QTIP, or to the QTIP trust). Thus, a general provision specifying that all taxes be paid by the estate is no longer sufficient to waive the right of recovery.

This change is effective for decedents dying after the date of enactment.

Accumulation Distributions (Throwback Rules)

Under prior law, the distribution of accumulated income from a complex trust to a beneficiary is subject to the throwback rules and property sold within two years of contribution is taxed at the contributor's marginal rate.

Under the new law, distributions from most domestic trusts (not foreign trusts) are exempt from the throwback rules. Certain domestic trusts created before March 1, 1984 which were created with a principal purpose of avoiding income tax may still be subject to the throwback rules. The special rule regarding property transferred to trusts and sold within two years of contribution has been repealed with respect to both domestic and foreign trusts.

This change is effective for distributions after the date of enactment.

Other Estate, Gift and Trust Modifications

Other estate, gift and trust provisions in the new tax law include:

- ❑ prohibition of revaluation of gifts for estate purposes after expiration of statute of limitations;
- ❑ exclusion from estate for qualified conservation easements;
- ❑ transitional rules under Section 2056A;
- ❑ treatment for estate tax purposes of short- term obligations held by non-resident aliens;

- ❏ treatment of pre-need funeral trusts;
- ❏ adjustments for gifts from revocable trusts within three years of decedent's death;
- ❏ clarification of treatment of survivor annuities under QTIP rules;
- ❏ treatment under QDOT rules of forms of ownership that are not trusts;
- ❏ opportunity to correct special use valuation elections;
- ❏ authority to waive requirement of U.S. trustee for QDOTs;
- ❏ treatment of certain rents under special valuation rules;
- ❏ declaratory judgments relating to value of certain gifts.

Coopers & Lybrand L.L.P.

International

The international provisions include several long-awaited simplification measures and a number of technical changes. Among the most significant international changes included in the legislation—and the most costly—deal with the export of computer software, joint venture companies and the special income exclusion for expatriates.

Foreign Simplification and Other Foreign Provisions Affecting Businesses and Individuals with Activities Outside the United States

Foreign Sales Corporations

IRS regulations take the position that computer software is not export property eligible for foreign sales corporation (FSC) benefits unless the product cannot be copied for resale. The regulations classified it under the statutory exclusion that applies to intangible property other than films, tapes, records or similar reproductions for commercial or home use.

Congress now recognizes that, because of technological developments, computer software is basically indistinguishable from films, tapes and records, which may be exported through a FSC. Under the new law, computer software (whether or not patented) is eligible as export property for FSC purposes, and Congress intends that the term be construed broadly to accommodate future technological developments.

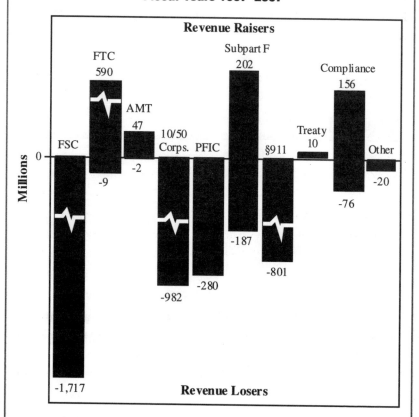

International Provisions — Revenue Estimates
Fiscal Years 1997–2007

Source: Estimated budget effects of "The Taxpayer Relief Act of 1997,"
Joint Committee on Taxation (July 30, 1997).

The change applies to gross receipts from computer software licenses in tax
years ending after December 31, 1997.

> **Observation:** The treatment of computer software for FSC purposes has
> been controversial. Several major manufacturers argued in litigation that
> computer software qualifies as export property. In making the change,
> Congress intends no inference should be drawn with respect to the treat-
> ment of computer software under the prior law.

Coopers & Lybrand L.L.P.

Foreign Tax Credit Rules

Translation and Redeterminations of Foreign Taxes

One of the more burdensome international provisions included in the Tax Reform Act of 1986 required that creditable foreign income taxes be translated into U.S. dollars at the exchange rate applicable on the date the taxes are actually paid. Businesses have strongly recommended that the rule be changed, and every international simplification bill sent to the President in recent years has included a change to this rule.

The new law generally requires that foreign income taxes be translated into U.S. dollars at the average exchange rate for the tax year to which they relate. Exceptions apply to taxes paid two or more years after the close of a tax year and taxes paid prior to the year to which they relate, as well as tax payments denominated in hyperinflationary currencies. Under the new law, these taxes are translated into U.S. dollars generally using the exchange rate applicable to the payment date; however, the IRS may issue regulations to require the use of an average exchange rate for a specified period. This change is effective for taxes paid or accrued in tax years beginning after December 31, 1997.

The new law requires that taxpayers notify the IRS when accrued foreign taxes in U.S. dollars differ from the amount paid or when accrued taxes remain unpaid for more than two years after the close of the tax year to which they relate. Notification is also required when there is a refund of foreign taxes.

The IRS can redetermine the amount of taxes for the years affected or adjust the pools of taxes and undistributed earnings. The new law affirms the IRS's authority to make adjustments prospectively in lieu of requiring the redetermination of foreign tax credits.

Credit Below the Third Tier

Under prior law, a U.S. shareholder of a foreign corporation, which is owned through a foreign ownership chain, could not receive a foreign tax credit (FTC) for the taxes paid by that foreign corporation if a dividend was paid through more than two foreign corporations; in other words, a deemed-paid credit was not available for taxes paid below the third-tier. The same rule applied in the case of FTCs associated with subpart F inclusions.

This limitation imposed a significant burden on U.S. businesses that acquired foreign operations with complex ownership chains. The FTC ownership requirements limited the flexibility of U.S. corporations to establish foreign holding company structures for tax or business reasons.

The new law extends the application of the FTC to certain taxes paid or accrued by certain fourth-, fifth- and sixth-tier foreign corporations. To be eligible, a foreign corporation below the third-tier paying the tax must be a controlled foreign corporation (CFC) and the corporation claiming the credit must be a U.S. shareholder (10-percent owner) of the CFC. In addition, the direct and indirect ownership percentage of voting stock down the chain, when multiplied, must be at least 5 percent.

The change applies to foreign taxes paid or incurred with respect to a CFC's tax years beginning after the date of enactment. Under prior law, ownership was tested on the date of distribution, and it was possible that restructuring might permit an FTC even though the foreign taxes were paid or incurred by a foreign corporation below the third-tier. It is important to note that the new law denies an FTC if the ownership requirements are met on the date of distribution because of a liquidation, reorganization or similar transaction in a tax year beginning after the date of enactment.

New Holding Period

Although a holding period requirement applies for purposes of the dividend-received deduction for corporate shareholders, prior law did not impose a similar requirement on the foreign tax credit associated with dividend distributions. The new law denies a shareholder the foreign tax credit normally available with respect to a dividend from a foreign corporation or regulated investment company if the shareholder has not held the stock for a minimum period. The new requirement applies both to the FTC for withholding taxes and the deemed-paid credit applicable to dividends and subpart F inclusions. The new holding period requirement is effective 30 days after enactment.

The FTC holding period is 16 days for common stock, measured during the 30-day period beginning 15 days before the stock becomes ex-dividend. For preferred stock and dividends attributable to a period or periods aggregating in excess of 366 days, the holding period is 46 days measured during a 90 day period beginning 45 days before the shareholder becomes entitled to receive a dividend. Any period during which the shareholder is protected from risk of loss does not apply for purposes of these tests. The new law includes an exception for certain active dealers in securities.

If the holding period is not met, the new law permits a deduction for taxes that would otherwise be creditable.

Interest on Underpayments

If a foreign tax credit carryback results in an *overpayment* of tax, the overpayment is deemed to arise when the return is filed for the year that generated the carryback claim. Thus, interest does not accrue on the overpayment prior to the filing date for the year that effectively created the overpayment. In *Fluor v. U.S.*, the court concluded that interest does not accrue on an *underpayment* by the taxpayer that is eliminated by an FTC carryback.

Congress believes that the application of the interest rules in the case of a deficiency that is reduced or eliminated by an FTC carryback should be consistent with rules that apply to overpayments. Under the new law, a carryback will not affect the computation of interest on underpayments for the period ending with the filing date in the subsequent year when the foreign taxes are paid or accrued.

Period of Limitations

Under prior law, overpayments attributable to foreign tax credits are subject to a 10-year period of limitation for the filing date for the tax year with respect to which the claim is made. In the case of an FTC carryforward, the IRS has determined the period of limitation by reference to the year in which the foreign taxes were paid or accrued. In *Ampex Corp. v. U.S.*, however, the court concluded that the period of limitation is determined by reference to the year to which the FTC is carried. The new law codifies the IRS's position. Thus, in a claim for overpayment attributable to FTCs, the limitation period is determined by reference to the year the foreign taxes were paid or accrued. The provision is effective for foreign taxes paid or accrued in tax years beginning after the date of enactment.

AMT Changes

To determine the FTC that can be claimed currently, expenses must be allocated and apportioned to a U.S. taxpayer's foreign source-income to determine the foreign tax credit limitation. A separate limitation must be computed for purposes of the regular tax and for the alternative minimum tax (AMT). Under the new law, taxpayers can elect to use the ratio of foreign-source, regular taxable income to AMT income as the AMT foreign tax credit limitation, provided foreign-source, regular taxable income does not exceed AMT income. The election must be made for the first tax year beginning after December 31, 1997, for which an AMT foreign tax credit is claimed. Once made, the election can only be revoked with the consent of the Secretary of the Treasury.

In general, the only tax credit fully allowed to compute the AMT is the alternative minimum tax foreign tax credit, which may be no higher than 90 percent of the tentative minimum tax. Prior law, however, provided an exception that allowed a limited number of domestic corporations to claim 100 percent of their AMT foreign tax credit.

The new law repeals the 100-percent exception, and the change applies to tax years beginning after the date of enactment.

Other Changes

The new law clarifies that a foreign corporation's post-1986 foreign income tax pool includes only those taxes that are not attributable to dividends distributed in prior years.

A proposal that would have shortened the FTC carryback period and lengthened the carryforward period was included in the Senate package, but the proposed change was not included in the new law.

The new law does not include a proposed change the would change the source of income with respect to certain inventory sales between U.S. residents that occur outside the United States.

Joint Ventures
10/50 Basket
Dividends paid by each noncontrolled foreign corporation in which a U.S. shareholder has an interest are subject to a separate foreign tax credit limitation or basket. (A non-controlled foreign corporation (10/50) is a foreign corporation in which a U.S. shareholder owns 10 percent or more of the voting shares and not more than 50 percent of the vote or value.) Any excess foreign tax credits (or excess limitation) in a 10/50 basket cannot be used to benefit another basket, including baskets for dividends from other 10/50 companies. This treatment imposed a significant record-keeping and compliance burden on businesses, and it might discourage foreign joint ventures.

> **Observation:** To avoid 10/50 basket limitations, U.S. companies have attempted structuring investments through foreign entities that are treated as CFCs or partnerships for U.S. tax purposes. Even with the new "check-the-box" regulations, it is not always possible to easily achieve this result.

Under the new law, a single foreign tax credit limitation category will apply to non-PFIC 10/50 companies effective for earnings accumulated before December 31, 2002.

Special look-through rules apply to post-2002 earnings distributions. After the repeal is effective, dividends from 10/50 companies generally will be basketed under look-through rules like those applicable to dividends from CFCs. Thus, the 10/50 basket is effectively repealed for post-2002 earnings.

Observation: Look-through treatment for 10/50 companies has not been extended to include interest, rents and royalties.

The new law also repeals the general inclusion in the 10/50 basket of dividends paid by a CFC from earnings accrued before the recipient shareholder became a U.S. shareholder. The application of the look-through rule in such circumstances is effective for distributions after the date of enactment.

Repeal of Excise Tax

Under prior law, an excise tax was imposed on U.S. persons that made contributions to the capital (or paid-in surplus) of a foreign corporation or that transferred property to a foreign partnership, estate or trust. Unless an exception applied, the Section 1491 tax was 35 percent of the inherent tax gain in the property transferred. A substantial penalty could apply if a transfer subject to Section 1491 was not reported. Section 367 applies to certain transfers by U.S. persons to foreign corporations and, frequently, requires gain recognition with respect to the property transferred.

Congress recognizes that these excise tax rules could operate as a trap for the unwary, and, effective upon enactment, the new law repeals them and Section 1057, which permitted an alternative exchange treatment for transfers subject to Section 1491. Under the new law, gain recognition is required when appreciated property is transferred to a foreign estate or trust (but generally not a partnership). In addition, regulations are authorized under Section 367 to deny nonrecognition treatment to certain transfers to foreign corporations and to require gain recognition on a transfer of appreciated property to a foreign partnership when the inherent gain would be transferred to a foreign partner.

Residence of Partnerships

A partnership is considered to be a domestic partnership if it is created or organized in the United States or under the laws of the United States or any state. A foreign partnership is generally any partnership that is not a domestic partnership. The new law authorizes regulations to treat a partnership that would otherwise be domestic as a foreign partnership instead where such treatment is more appropriate. Congress expects that the regulations will consider such material factors as the residence of the partners, the extent to which

Coopers & Lybrand L.L.P.

the partnership is engaged in business in the United States and the source of the income it earns. In addition, regulations will provide additional guidance to determine whether a partnership for tax purposes is domestic or foreign. Regulations issued under the new law will apply to partnerships organized or created after regulations or a notice are issued.

> **Observation:** In authorizing regulations, Congress is dealing with at least two issues. First, Congress is authorizing regulations that respond to comments made with respect to the proposed check-the-box regulations. Commentators requested guidance on the classification of certain arrangements classified as a partnership under U.S. tax rules. Second, the new law authorizes the IRS to address the classification of partnerships initially organized overseas and later domesticated.

Anti-Deferral Changes

Sales of CFC Shares

When a controlled foreign corporation (CFC) sells shares in a lower-tier CFC, the gain is taxable generally to the CFC's U.S. shareholder as passive basket subpart F income, and the U.S. shareholder's basis in the upper-tier CFC is increased by the amount of subpart F income recognized. On the other hand, if a U.S. shareholder sells shares in an upper-tier CFC, gain on the sale is treated as dividend income under Sec. 1248 to the extent of the earnings and profits of the foreign corporation. In addition, the U.S. shareholder can claim a foreign tax credit attributable to the deemed dividend, which is characterized on a look-through basis for FTC limitation purposes.

Upon enactment, the new law treats the gain on the sale or exchange of stock by a CFC in any other foreign corporation as dividend income to the same extent that it would have been dividend income to a U.S. person under Section 1248 if the foreign corporation were sold by its U.S. shareholder. (As a general rule, Section 1248 applies only to the sale of a CFC.) The amount characterized as dividend income (and eligible for look-through treatment) under the new law generally will be taxable currently under the subpart F rules applicable to dividend distributions (applied without regard to the same country exception).

In addition, the new law authorizes regulations to permit a CFC's basis in shares of another CFC to be increased for undistributed previously taxed income that is taxable to its U.S. shareholder. These changes are effective for tax years of U.S. shareholders beginning after December 31, 1997.

PFICs

The passive foreign investment company (PFICs) regime was established by the Tax Reform Act of 1986, and Congress intended that it would eliminate the benefits of deferral with respect to foreign corporations that were not CFCs. A PFIC is any foreign corporation, in which a U.S. person has a direct or indirect stock interest, that earns a significant amount of passive income or holds a majority of passive assets.

U.S. owners must include their pro rata share of the foreign corporation's earnings in gross income under the qualified electing fund (QEF) option or pay tax on the PFIC's deemed or actual distributions and an interest charge that is attributable to the value of the U.S. tax deferral.

Formerly, U.S. shareholders of CFCs that were also PFICs could be subject both to the subpart F provisions and the PFIC interest charge rules.

Under the new law, a PFIC that is also a CFC will not be a PFIC with respect to 10-percent U.S. shareholders, determined under the subpart F rules. Thus, a U.S. shareholder of a CFC will not be subject both to the current inclusion rules under subpart F and the non-QEF PFIC rules. The new rule applies to post-1997 holding periods; however, a U.S. shareholder can eliminate the PFIC taint for prior earnings by making an election to pay tax and an interest charge with respect to the unrealized appreciation in the stock or the accumulated earnings of the foreign corporation.

Under prior law, it was difficult for portfolio investors to elect QEF status with respect to their investments because the U.S. earnings and profits of the foreign corporation were not readily ascertainable. The new law provides a mark-to-market election, which cannot be revoked without permission, for marketable shares in PFICs. Thus, electing U.S. shareholders can avoid the interest-charge rules applicable to PFICs that are not QEFs.

Electing U.S. shareholders (and certain electing CFCs) must annually include as ordinary income (or foreign personal holding company income in the case of a CFC) an amount equal to the excess of the fair market value of the PFIC stock as of the close of the tax year over the basis in the shares, adjusted for amounts previously taxed to the shareholder. An ordinary deduction is available if the adjusted basis in the shares is greater than the fair market value, but only to the extent of any prior years' unreversed mark-to-market inclusions. Ordinary gains or loss treatment also applies with respect to the actual disposition of electing PFIC shares.

The new election applies to marketable shares and options regularly traded on national exchanges or national market system. In addition, PFIC shares are considered marketable if they are regularly traded and the Secretary of the Treasury determines that the market price represents fair market value or their value can be determined. Finally, the new law treats PFIC shares owned by a regulated investment company (RIC) as marketable if the RIC offers for sale (or has outstanding) stock that is redeemable at its net asset value or publishes the net asset valuations of the PFIC shares at least annually. Special rules apply in the treatment of the mark-to-market income under RIC rules.

U.S. persons owning PFIC shares through foreign partnerships or trusts are treated under the new law as proportionally owning the PFIC shares. A disposition of the ownership interest in the partnership or trust (or its interest in the PFIC) is treated as a PFIC disposition.

The new law also makes a change to the rules that apply to the measurement of assets for purposes of applying the PFIC asset test. If the stock of a foreign corporation is publicly traded, the PFIC asset test is to be applied using the fair market value of assets. Congress intends that the total value of a publicly traded foreign corporation's assets generally will be treated as equal to the sum of the aggregate value of its outstanding stock plus liabilities.

The new PFIC rules are effective for tax years of U.S. persons beginning after December 31, 1997, and tax years of foreign corporations ending with or within such tax years.

Subpart F Changes

When a U.S. shareholder acquires the stock of a CFC during the foreign corporation's tax year, the new 10-percent shareholder is taxed on a pro-rata share of the foreign corporation's subpart F income, reduced by all or a portion of the amount of actual dividends paid by the CFC to any other shareholder. The new law also reduces the new shareholder's subpart F income by treating the Section 1248 deemed dividend like an actual dividend paid that is paid to the seller. This change is effective with respect to acquisitions occurring after the date of enactment.

Foreign passive type income earned through a foreign corporation is generally foreign personal holding company (FPHC) income that is taxable under subpart F. For tax years beginning after the date of enactment, the new law treats net income from all types of notional principal contracts as FPHC income and includes it in a new category, unless it is a hedge of an item in another category of FPHC income. Payments in lieu of dividends derived from equity securities lending transactions are another new category of FPHC income. Finally, the new law provides an exemption from FPHC income for amounts resulting from transactions entered into in the ordinary course of a CFC's business as a regular dealer in property, forward contracts, options, notional principal contracts, or similar financial instruments (including instruments referenced to commodities).

The new law provides an exception from FPHC income for certain income derived in the active conduct of an insurance, banking, financing or similar business. In the case of insurance companies, the new law excludes certain investment income associated with same-country risks from subpart F. Complex rules apply to determine whether the CFC is genuinely conducting such a business. The exception, however, is applicable only for tax years beginning in 1998. Anti-abuse rules will apply to transactions that are intended to accelerate or defer any item in order to claim the benefit of the new rules.

> **Observation:** The change, permitting deferral for these industries, is significant even if it applies only for one year. The conferees recognized

that this area requires further study and may evaluate this measure in the future and invite comments regarding the complex issues involved.

Certain investments in U.S. property by a CFC can result in a deemed dividend to the foreign corporation's U.S. shareholders under Section 956. The new law provides two additional exceptions from the definition of U.S. property. Both exceptions relate to transactions entered into by securities or commodities dealers in the ordinary course of business. Under the new law, customary deposits of collateral or margin by these dealers are not taxable as Section 956 investments. The second exception applies to repurchase agreement transactions and reverse repurchase agreements. These changes are effective for tax years of foreign corporations beginning after December 31, 1997.

Subpart F income does not include U.S.-source income that is also effectively connected with the conduct of a U.S. trade or business, provided the CFC's income is not exempt from or subject to a reduced rate of tax under an income tax treaty. The new law clarifies when the treaty rule applies—an elimination or reduction by treaty of the branch profits tax does not terminate the exemption from subpart F for determinations made in tax years beginning after December 31, 1986.

> Observation: Since this change is retroactive, U.S. shareholders of CFC that have reported effectively connected income as subpart F income based on the treatment of the branch profits tax under an treaty should amend the affected income tax returns.

Foreign Transfers

A special rule applies when intangibles are contributed to a foreign corporation in what would otherwise be a tax-free exchange. Under Section 367(d), the U.S. contributor is treated as having sold the property in exchange for a deemed U.S.-source royalty payment from the transferee foreign corporation. The new law provides that the deemed royalty under Section 367(d) is foreign-source income if an actual royalty payment for the intangible would be considered foreign source. Congress also authorized regulations to require similar treatment in the case of a transfer of intangible property to a foreign partnership. The new sourcing rule is effective for transfers made and royalties deemed received after the date of enactment.

Compliance Provisions

Information Reporting

In the case of foreign partnerships, a U.S. return is required generally if the partnership had U.S.-source income or was engaged in a U.S. trade or businesses. The new law clarifies that deductions (as well as losses and credits) will not be available with respect to certain foreign partnerships that do not file the required returns.

Controlling U.S. partners (and controlling 10 percent partners) are also required under the new law to file annual information returns with respect to foreign partnerships, as well as disclose changes in ownership. The provision authorizing disclosure on Form 5471 has been expanded to apply to foreign partnerships as well as foreign corporations. A penalty of $10,000 applies to a failure to comply with the new reporting requirements, and an additional penalty up to $50,000 applies in the case of continued noncompliance after notification.

Transfers to foreign partnerships must now be reported on information returns if the U.S. transferor owns a 10-percent-or-more interest in the partnership or the value of the property transferred in a 12-month period exceeds $100,000. A penalty of 10 percent of the value of the property transferred applies if the transfer is not reported, and the U.S. transferor must recognize gain on the property transferred. The penalty for any exchange shall not exceed $100,000, unless the failure was due to intentional disregard. (Transfers to foreign corporations are now also subject to a 10-percent penalty). The new rules apply as of the date of enactment; however, a retroactive election to August 20, 1996, is available for transfers to foreign partnerships.

Extended Statute of Limitation

Under the new law, a failure to file returns or report required information with respect to a transfer to a foreign corporation, partnership or trust will extend the statute of limitation with respect to any event or period to which such

Coopers & Lybrand L.L.P.

information relates. It will not expire until three years after the date on which the information is provided. This modification is effective for information that must be reported after the date of enactment.

Reporting Threshold

Certain shareholders and directors of foreign corporations must file information returns (Form 5471) on behalf of such corporations. Under Section 6046, a triggering event occurs when a U.S. person acquires 5-percent or more of the value of the stock of a foreign corporation (or becomes a U.S. person holding such an ownership interest). U.S. citizens and residents that are officers and directors of foreign corporations who own 5-percent interest must also file information returns. Congress was concerned that the 5-percent ownership interest did not parallel the 10-percent ownership thresholds that apply to Form 5471. The new law increases the Section 6046 reporting percentage to a 10-percent vote or value test. This amendment is effective as of January 1, 1998.

Individuals

Section 911 Exclusion

The foreign earned income exclusion for U.S. individuals working abroad has been characterized by some groups as corporate welfare. Congress believes that the Section 911 exclusion helps to ameliorate the inequitable tax burden placed on U.S. individuals working abroad.

Beginning in 1998, the new law increases the foreign earned income exclusion from $70,000 in annual increments of $2,000 until it reaches $80,000 in 2002. In 2008, the Section 911 exclusion will be indexed for inflation after the year 2006.

Simplified FTC Limitation

In 1986, Congress expanded the number of limitation categories (or baskets) that apply to the computation of the foreign tax credit, and those rules apply to individual and corporate taxpayers. Under these rules, income and taxes attributable to passive-type investments (for example, interest and portfolio dividends) generally are basketed separately from the income and taxes associated with other types of income. These changes were intended to make it more difficult for businesses (and individuals) to use the foreign tax credit to reduce their U.S. tax by making tax-motivated investments. Separate limitation categories increase the compliance burden on U.S. taxpayers; in the case of U.S. individuals making minimal investments offshore, the burden is not warranted. The new law allows individuals with no more than $300 ($600 in the case of persons filing joint returns) of creditable foreign taxes to elect to be exempt from the separate limitation rules, provided that they do not earn income other than qualified passive income and they receive a payee statement reporting the foreign-source income and taxes. Carryovers of excess foreign tax credits by electing shareholders will not be allowed, and the special rules are not available to estates or trusts. The new law applies to tax years beginning after December 31, 1997.

De Minimis Foreign Currency Gains

If a U.S. individual converts U.S. dollars to a foreign currency for personal use, such as those that do not result in a tax deduction, a taxable exchange gain (or a loss) can result when any remaining foreign currency is reconverted to U.S. dollars. The new law applies nonrecognition treatment to gains resulting from exchange rate changes between the acquisition and disposition of a foreign currency, provided personal gains (and certain business travel gains) do not exceed $200. The new law does not change the treatment of an individual's personal losses that generally are not deductible for tax purposes.

Like-Kind Exchanges of Foreign Property

The new law provides that property used predominantly within the United States and property used predominantly outside the United States are not

Coopers & Lybrand L.L.P.

"like-kind" properties for purposes of the nonrecognition rules of Section 1031. The situs of property for this purpose is determined generally using a two-year period before and after the exchange. The new rule is effective generally for transfers made after June 8, 1997, unless a binding contract is in effect on that date.

Certain Outbound Transfers of Property

The new law now requires gain recognition upon the transfer of appreciated property by a U.S. person to a foreign estate or nongrantor trust. Gain recognition also applies when a domestic trust becomes a foreign trust. In making this change, Congress repealed the excise tax rules under Sections 1491–94 previously applied to such transfers. In addition, the new law authorizes regulations that would deny the nonrecognition treatment that is provided under Section 1035 to certain exchanges of insurance policies, where the transferee is a foreign person.

Grantor Trust Changes

Legislation enacted in 1996 changed the rules applicable to determining the residence of a trust for tax purposes. As a result, trusts that qualified as U.S. trusts under prior law could fail to qualify under the 1996 rules. Under a technical correction in the new law, regulations will be issued to permit nongrantor trusts to elect to be treated as U.S. trusts. The change applies to tax years beginning after December 31, 1996.

Inbound Investors

Limitation on Treaty Benefits

Dividends, interest and other types of passive U.S.-source income paid to foreign persons are subject to 30-percent withholding; however, income tax treaties generally reduce or eliminate this gross tax if the income is paid to a resident of the treaty country.

In June 1997, the IRS issued temporary regulations to determine whether U.S.-source payments made to entities, including entities that are transparent for tax purposes in the United States and/or the applicable treaty jurisdiction are eligible for reduced withholding rates under an income tax treaty. The regulations were intended to clarify the rules applicable to these fiscally transparent entities, including hybrid entities that are treated as fiscally transparent by one, but not both, of the treaty partners. The regulations would deny treaty benefits to any foreign person that invests in the United States through a U.S. or foreign hybrid. The regulations apply on a prospective basis to amounts paid after December 31, 1997.

Both the House and Senate versions of the tax bill contained measures that would apply to the treatment of these entities under treaties. Under the conference agreement, income paid to an entity that is treated as a partnership (or is otherwise treated as fiscally transparent) for U.S. tax purposes is not entitled to a reduced rate of withholding under a treaty if:

❑ the income is not treated as income of the treaty resident under foreign country laws;
❑ the foreign country does not impose tax on an actual distribution of the income from the entity to a treaty resident; and
❑ the treaty itself does not contain a provision addressing the treatment of income derived through a partnership or other fiscally transparent entity.

In addition, the new law grants regulatory authority for the IRS to issue guidance in other situations where a treaty benefits should not apply with respect to payments received by, or income attributable to activities of, an entity that is treated as a partnership for U.S. tax purposes and is not treated as fiscally transparent in the foreign jurisdiction. Finally, the conference agreement indicates the belief that the new law and the recently issued regulations are consistent with U.S. treaties. The new provision is effective on date of enactment.

Elimination of Principal Office Requirement

Nonresident individuals and foreign corporations can qualify for a safe-harbor rule to trade in stocks or securities for their own account within the United States without the income being taxed as effectively connected with a U.S. trade or business. To qualify for the safe harbor, a foreign corporation or securities trading partnership cannot be a dealer in stocks and securities. In addition, such investor must maintain its "principal office" outside of the United States. Treasury regulations look to where various routine operations are performed to determine the situs of the principal office; the location of the entity's management or where investment decisions are made are not considered.

For partnerships and foreign corporations that trade stock or securities for their own account the new law eliminates the offshore principal office requirement. This change should reduce the complexity (and costs) associated with maintaining a foreign office. The provision is effective for tax years beginning after December 31, 1997.

Pass-Through Entities

Partnerships

Allocation of Basis to Distributed Properties

Partners generally may receive distributions of partnership property (other than money or marketable securities) without recognizing gain or loss. Similarly, property distributions are tax-free to the distributing partnership.

Two different rules determine a distributee partner's basis in distributed property, depending on whether the distribution is in liquidation of the distributee's interest in the partnership.

Normally, in a nonliquidating distribution, a distributee partner takes a carryover basis in distributed partnership property equal to the partnership's basis. This carryover basis, however, may not exceed the distributee's partnership interest basis. In contrast, generally a distributee partner's partnership interest basis is substituted for the basis of property received in a liquidating distribution.

Under prior law, an allocation rule was used when multiple properties were distributed to a partner in either a liquidating distribution or a non-liquidating distribution in which the total carryover basis of the distributed property exceeded the partner's interest basis. Partnership interest basis was first allocated to unrealized receivables and inventory (to the extent of the partnership's basis in those assets) and then to the remaining assets distributed in proportion to their respective bases to the partnership. Through this method (which completely ignored fair market value), it was possible for the distributee partner to have a higher basis in certain distributed property than the partnership had in the same property.

> **Observation:** Prior law often produced unusual results. Since fair market value was ignored, a distributee's basis was often allocated to low-value assets with basis, while no basis attached to the high value, zero basis assets received. This process often led to the so-called "million dollar typewriter."

Under the new law, the distributee partner's basis in his partnership interest is allocated first to unrealized receivables and inventory. If allocable basis is less than the partnership's basis in the distributed unrealized receivables and inventory, the distributee's basis is allocable among these assets in proportion to the respective amounts of unrealized depreciation, and then in proportion to these assets' bases. If the distributee partner's allocable basis exceeds the basis the partnership had in the distributed unrealized receivables and inventory, that remaining basis is allocated among any other assets to the extent of the partnership's basis in those other assets. To the extent allocable basis exceeds the partnership's basis in the other distributed assets, it is allocated in relation to the unrealized appreciation in those assets. Finally, any remaining allocable basis is allocated among those assets based on their relative fair market values.

> **Example:** Partnership XYZ is owned equally by partners A, B and C. XYZ owns an intangible with a basis of $0 and a fair market value of $400, Machine 1 with a basis of $150 and a fair market value of $1,000 and Machine 2 with a basis of $75 and a fair market value of $100. Partner C has a basis of $200 in its partnership interest. The intangible and Machine 2 are distributed to Partner C in liquidation of its interest.

Under the prior law, although the intangible that Partner C received was 80 percent of the value of Partner C's distribution, Partner C had no basis in the intangible it received. Therefore, Partner C's entire $200 basis would have attached to Machine 2, giving Machine 2 a basis of $200—$100 in excess of

Coopers & Lybrand L.L.P.

its fair market value. Thus, Partner C could have recovered its basis over a shorter period than had basis been allocated to the amortizable intangible.

Under the new law, C's partnership interest basis would be allocated as follows: $75 to Machine 2 (an amount equal to XYZ's basis in Machine 2), $118 to the intangible ($400 of intangible appreciation divided by total appreciation in the distributed assets of $425, multiplied by C's $125 of remaining allocable basis), and $7 to Machine 2 ($25 of Machine 2 appreciation divided by total appreciation in the assets distributed of $425, multiplied by C's $125 of remaining allocable basis). Thus, Partner C's bases in its intangible and Machine 2 would be $118 and $82, respectively.

This change applies to partnership distributions made after the date of enactment.

Treatment of Inventory Items upon the Sale or Exchange of a Partnership Interest

The prior law required that any amount received upon the sale or exchange of a partnership interest that was attributable to unrealized receivables or "substantially appreciated inventory" was treated as an amount realized from selling an ordinary income asset. A similar rule applied to sales or exchanges caused by certain partnership distributions. Inventory was deemed to be substantially appreciated if its fair market value exceeded 120 percent of the partnership's basis in the inventory.

The new law deletes the requirement that inventory be substantially appreciated, but only when a partnership interest is sold or exchanged. Therefore, when a partnership interest is sold or exchanged and the partnership in which the interest is sold holds any appreciated inventory, a portion of any amount realized on the sale or exchange will be treated as ordinary income to the seller even if the partnership's inventory is not substantially appreciated.

The new law does not, however, change prior law's substantially appreciated inventory distribution rule.

> **Observation:** Presumably, Congress did not wish to increase the likelihood that a partnership distributee would be subject to the complexity

associated with characterizing a part of its distribution as sale or exchange as ordinary income. By removing the prior law's "substantially appreciated inventory" requirement for interest sales or exchanges, however, Congress has placed a premium on partnership redemptions when a partnership holds inventory that is not appreciated.

This change applies to sales of interests made after the date of enactment.

Treatment of Contributed Appreciated Property

Under prior law, if a partner contributed built-in gain or built-in loss property to a partnership and that property was distributed within five years to another partner, the contributor generally recognized such gain or loss as if the property had been sold for its fair market value at the time of the distribution. (These contributed property swaps were often referred to as "mixing bowl" transactions, see illustration below.) Similarly, if a partnership distributed appreciated property, other than that contributed, to a contributing partner, pre-contribution gain was recognized by the contributing partner to the extent of the lesser of precontribution gain or appreciation in the property on the distribution date.

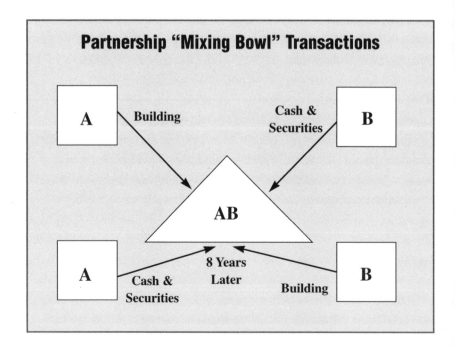

Partnership "Mixing Bowl" Transactions

A — Building → AB

B — Cash & Securities → AB

8 Years Later

A — Cash & Securities → AB

B — Building → AB

The new law increases the prior five-year "waiting period" to seven years and is effective for property contributions made after June 8, 1997. Contributed property subject to a written binding contract in effect on June 8, 1997, will continue to have a five-year waiting period.

> **Observation:** Prior law was enacted to prohibit abuse of the normal tax-free nature of partnership distributions. Congress was apparently concerned that the potential for abuse still existed so they extended the waiting period to seven years.

Publicly Traded Partnerships

A publicly traded partnership is a partnership whose interests are (1) traded on an established securities market, or (2) readily tradable on a secondary market (or the substantial equivalent thereof).

Publicly traded partnerships, with two exceptions, are treated as taxable corporations. The first exception is for entities otherwise satisfying the definition of publicly traded partnerships but 90 percent or more of whose gross income consists of "passive-type income." The second exception is for an "existing partnership" that was generally publicly traded on December 17, 1987. These publicly traded partnerships were granted grandfather status and were permitted to operate as partnerships, regardless of the nature of their income, for a 10-year period ending December 31, 1997. After December 31, 1997, these grandfathered publicly traded partnerships are automatically converted to C corporations.

Under the new law, effective for tax years beginning after December 31, 1997, if a grandfathered publicly traded partnership elects to be subject to a 3.5 percent tax on gross income from the active conduct of a trade or business, it may continue to be treated as a partnership. The partnership's gross trade or business income includes its share of gross trade or business income of any lower-tier partnership. The tax imposed under the provision may not be offset by tax credits.

Just as under prior law, a grandfathered publicly traded partnership that elects to pay the 3.5 percent tax will lose that election (and be treated as a corporation) if after December 31, 1997, it adds a substantial new line of business.

The election to be subject to the tax on gross trade or business income, once made, remains in effect until revoked by the partnership; once revoked, it cannot be reinstated.

> **Observation:** The tax on gross income is intended to approximate the corporate tax publicly traded partnerships would pay if they were treated as corporations for federal tax purposes. This tax does not apply to publicly traded partnerships that fall under the passive type income exception.

Simplified Flow-Through for Electing Large Partnerships

In general, most items of partnership income, gain, loss, deduction or credit are separately reported on Schedule K of the partnership tax return, and each partner's share of the item is shown on the Schedule K-1 furnished by the partnership to the partner (the Schedule K-1 contains space for more than 40 items). Each partner then is required to report separately in the partner's individual tax return the partner's distributive share of each item.

Reporting so many separately stated items can be burdensome for individual investors with relatively small, passive interests in large partnerships. Further, the number of items reported under the current regime makes it difficult for the IRS to match items reported on a Schedule K-1 against what a partner reports on its income tax return. Matching is also difficult because items on the K-1 are often modified or limited at the partner level before appearing on the partner's tax return.

For tax years beginning after December 31, 1997, to simplify reporting of partnership income, the new law reduces the number of items that must be separately reported to partners by an "electing large partnership." Generally, an electing large partnership is any partnership that elects simplified reporting under the provision and that has 100 or more partners in the tax year preceding its election. (Individual partners performing substantial personal services are generally not counted. Additionally, certain personal service partnerships are not allowed to make the election.) The new law provides that each partner only takes into account his or her distributive share of 11 specifically identified items, which are determined at the partnership level.

Coopers & Lybrand L.L.P.

Specifically Identified Separately Reportable Items of Electing Large Partnerships

❑ Taxable income or loss from passive loss limitation activities;

❑ Taxable income or loss from other activities (e.g., portfolio);

❑ Net capital gain or loss to the extent allocable to passive loss limitation activities and other activities;

❑ Tax-exempt interest;

❑ New alternative minimum tax adjustments separately computed for passive loss limitation activities and other activities;

❑ General credits;

❑ Low-income housing credit;

❑ Rehabilitation credit;

❑ Credit for producing fuel from a nonconventional source;

❑ Creditable foreign taxes and foreign-source items;

❑ Any other items to the extent the IRS determines that separate treatment of such items is appropriate.

The taxable income of an electing large partnership is computed in the same manner as that of an individual, except that the items described above are separately stated and certain modifications are made. These modifications include disallowing the deduction for personal exemptions, the net operating loss deduction and certain itemized deductions. All limitations and other provisions affecting the computation of taxable income or any credit (except for the at- risk, passive loss and itemized deduction limitations, and any other provision specified in regulations) are applied at the partnership (and not the partner) level.

All elections affecting the computation of taxable income or any credit generally are made by the partnership.

Closing of Partnership Tax Year for Deceased Partner

Prior law provided that a partnership tax year closed for a partner whose entire interest was sold, exchanged or liquidated. A partnership's tax year generally did not close, however, upon the death of a partner. Accordingly, a decedent's entire share of partnership items for the year of death was taxed to the decedent's estate or successor in interest rather than to the decedent on his or her final return.

The new law provides that the tax year of a partnership closes with respect to a partner whose partnership interest terminates by death.

This change applies to partnership tax years beginning after December 31, 1997.

Other Changes

The new law also:

❏ modifies investment company rules applicable to partnerships;
❏ modifies unified audit procedures;
❏ requires all partnerships with more than 100 partners to file their returns on magnetic media;
❏ clarifies when foreign partnerships are required to file returns; and
❏ authorizes Treasury to issue guidance for determining when a domestic partnership will be treated as a foreign partnership.

S Corporations

UBTI for S Corporation ESOPs

Tax law changes made in 1996 allow Employee Stock Option Plans (ESOPs), along with other tax-exempt organizations, to own S corporation stock for tax years beginning after December 31, 1997, without terminating the S corporation's status. At that time, the law also directed that all income allocated to the ESOP from the S corporation would be taxable as unrelated business taxable income (UBTI), common for other tax-exempt shareholders.

> Observation: The effect of this, however, put a double tax on the S corporation earnings attributable to the ESOP because participants in the ESOP are again taxed when distributions are made. The fact that the S corporation may or may not distribute all of the taxable income creates further problems for ESOPs when distributions must be made to plan participants.

Coopers & Lybrand

> **Example:** An ESOP owns 100 shares of an S corporation and is allocated $100,000 of taxable income over several years. The S corporation distributes to the ESOP only $50,000 (50% of the taxable income) for that period, and the ESOP pays a tax on its UBTI of $40,000 (40% combined federal and state marginal tax rate). To distribute the remaining $60,000 of increased value to plan participants, the ESOP must liquidate some of its holdings. Furthermore, the plan participants are then taxed on the $60,000 as ordinary income subject to the individual income tax rates, which can be as high as 39.6% for federal taxes. Plan participants would ultimately receive less than 50% of the S corporation earnings.

Although the effective date for this 1996 tax law change has not yet arrived, the new law repeals the UBTI on ESOP S corporation shareholders. Under the new law, an ESOP will not pay income tax on S corporation earnings allocated to it through stock ownership.

> **Observation:** This provision does not change the rules for other tax-exempt shareholders in S corporations. For those shareholders, S corporation income will continue to be UBTI.

The new law also includes some specific changes for S corporation ESOPs that allow cash distributions to shareholders and removes some restrictions on prohibited transactions. Both of these changes were required to make ESOPs practical for S corporations.

> **Observation:** This change now brings the ESOP back into the realm of possibilities for exit strategies for S corporation shareholders. Shareholders will be able to transfer their S corporations to employees through ESOPs without onerous UBTI.

The new law will take effect at the same time that ESOPs become eligible shareholders, which is tax years beginning after December 31, 1997.

Regulated Investment Companies

The new law repeals the 30-percent gross income requirement (the "short-3 test"), which limited the amount of realized gains that mutual funds could generate from the sale of securities held for less than three months. Repeal will provide mutual funds greater flexibility in the buying and selling of securities and in the use of futures and options to manage investment risk. This provision is effective for mutual funds' tax years beginning after the date of enactment.

The new law modifies the current safe harbor for stock and securities trading by eliminating the requirement that the principal office of offshore corporations and partnerships trading stock and securities for their own account be located outside the United States. This legislation will significantly impact the hedge fund industry by eliminating the need to maintain an office offshore, resulting in a reduction of the costs and complexities associated with the maintenance of offshore funds. This provision is effective for tax years beginning after December 31, 1997.

Real Estate Investment Trusts

The new law also includes a series of twelve real estate investment trust (REIT) simplification provisions that fit into three broad categories: three provisions eliminating unnecessary tax traps that could have resulted in a loss of REIT status; two provisions that bring further conformity to the rules that govern REITs and Regulated Investment Companies (i.e., mutual funds); and a series of provisions simplifying the formation or operation of a REIT. All changes to the REIT rules are effective for tax years beginning after the date of enactment.

Shareholder Demand Letters

Two significant changes are: (1) a REIT is no longer subject to disqualification for failing to comply with the requirements of the demand letter regulations (which are designed to ascertain ownership in the REIT); and (2) a REIT that does comply with the regulations will be deemed to satisfy the REIT closely held ownership test if it does not know or have reason to know that it did not meet the ownership test.

Coopers & Lybrand L.L.P.

In the event that a REIT fails to comply with the regulations, the IRS is permitted to: (1) require that the REIT take actions to ascertain its ownership for the affected period; and (2) impose a $25,000 penalty unless the REIT shows that its failure to comply was a result of reasonable cause. If the REIT is found to have intentionally disregarded the requirements set out in the regulations, a $50,000 penalty is imposed. Also, if a REIT fails to act to rectify its noncompliance upon a request of the IRS, a second set of penalties equal to the first will be imposed.

De Minimis Income from Impermissible Tenant Services

Prior law provided that for purposes of the REIT gross income tests, a REIT could disqualify all amounts received from a tenant if the REIT furnished any "impermissible service" to that tenant. In general, an impermissible service is defined as a service not customarily furnished by landlords of comparable properties or that is furnished primarily for the convenience of a tenant (e.g., maid service for apartment tenants).

Under the new law, a REIT may provide a *de minimis* level of impermissible services to a tenant without affecting the qualification of the rents paid by the tenant. The gross income received by a REIT in exchange for an impermissible tenant service continues to represent nonqualifying REIT income. However, the character of otherwise qualifying amounts received from a tenant (e.g., rent) will not be affected unless more than 1 percent of a REIT's total gross income from a property is comprised of income related to impermissible tenant services. If the 1-percent threshold is exceeded, all amounts received from a tenant will become nonqualifying REIT income.

> **Observation:** This change not only nearly eliminates the possibility of a REIT losing its status as a result of employees inadvertently performing unauthorized services to a tenant, but provides a REIT with an opportunity to actively provide a small level of impermissible services to tenants.

> **Observation:** Under prior law, it appeared that an impermissible service to one tenant would not impact upon the qualification of amounts received from other tenants. However, because the new law's 1-percent threshold is based upon the gross income from each property, a REIT

may taint amounts received from all tenants of a property if the REIT exceeds the 1-percent gross income threshold, even though the impermissible service income may relate only to certain tenants of that property.

With respect to the amount a REIT receives for furnishing an impermissible service, the new law mandates that the amount may not be less than 150 percent of the direct cost to the REIT of furnishing such service.

Credit for Tax Paid on Retained Capital Gains

Under the new law (which conforms the REIT rules to existing rules for mutual funds), a REIT will now be permitted to pass through to shareholders a credit for any tax a REIT pays when it retains capital gains. By providing shareholders with a credit for the tax paid by the REIT, capital gains retained by a REIT will be subject only to one level of tax (at the shareholder level upon their eventual distribution to shareholders). Under prior law, capital gains that were retained by a REIT were subject to a tax at both the REIT and shareholder level.

Repeal of the 30-Percent Gross Income Requirement

Prior law provided that no more than 30 percent of a REIT's gross income could result from gains attributable to sales of dealer property, real estate assets held for less than four years or stock or other securities held for less than one year. This gross income test has been repealed. However, the prohibited transaction test, which precludes a REIT from becoming a dealer in property, will continue to limit a REIT's sales activities.

Other Changes

❏ The new law reduces the chance that a REIT or its shareholders may inappropriately be attributed ownership, via complex ownership attribution rules, in a tenant of the REIT or an entity seeking to act as an independent contractor to the REIT.

❏ New law reverses the order in which a REIT is deemed to distribute E&P. Now a REIT's first distributions, following the acquisition of C corporation E&P (via a merger or REIT election), will be deemed to carry out the C corporation E&P. This change significantly reduces any chance for a REIT to be disqualified for failing to distribute C corporation earnings in the year the earnings are acquired.

❏ The foreclosure property election period is lengthened to three years (but now only one extension is permitted). REITs may now terminate the election, and the ability granted to REITs in 1986 to provide certain usual and customary services in connection with the lease of real property, without the use of an independent contractor, is extended to foreclosure property.

❏ The REIT hedging provision, which under prior law applied only to hedges of variable rate debt, has been modified to include amounts received with respect to any hedge of a REIT liability secured by real property or used to acquire or improve real property.

❏ The new law expands the forms of phantom (non-cash) income that can be excluded from the REIT 95 percent income distribution requirement. Keep in mind, however, that the REIT must pay tax on any forms of phantom income it excludes from the distribution requirement.

❏ The prohibited transaction tax safe harbor is made easier to satisfy by no longer counting involuntary conversions against the seven sales of property allowed for each tax year.

❏ In narrow but important changes related to shared appreciation mortgages: (1) a REIT generally will not be subject to the prohibited transactions tax if property securing the mortgage is disposed of due to the mortgagor's bankruptcy; and (2) amounts received by a REIT that are attributable to an appreciation in a property's value will represent qualifying income.

❏ Under the new law, any corporation wholly owned by a REIT is treated as a qualified REIT subsidiary, regardless of whether the corporation has always been wholly owned by the REIT.

Procedural Provisions

Partnership Audit Procedures

Under prior law, all partnerships except those with 10 or fewer partners, each of whom is a natural person (other than a nonresident alien) or an estate, are subject to the unified audit rules. Under those rules, all partnership items are determined at the entity, rather than individual partner, level. If a partner takes a position inconsistent with that of the partnership, absent notification, the IRS can make a computational adjustment and immediately assess any resulting tax. If the IRS challenges a partnership reporting position, it must do so through an entity-level proceeding, even though any resulting adjustments to the partners' tax returns must be assessed at the individual level.

The new law generally continues this overall system with two important modifications. First, the exclusion of small partnerships (10 or fewer partners) from the entity-level rules now applies to partnerships with corporate partners, unless such treatment is specifically elected. This rule applies to partnership tax years ending after the date of enactment.

Second, subject to a special exclusion for service partners, partnerships with 100 or more partners in the preceding partnership tax year can elect a new audit regime (electing large partnerships). Under the new system, partnership adjustments are taken into account in computing partners' shares of partnership items for the current year (i.e., the partnership's tax year in which the adjustment takes effect) rather than adjusting the shares of partners in the partnership in the year or years actually under exam. In lieu of this approach, a further election can be made by this type of partnership to pay an imputed underpayment. The imputed underpayment is calculated by netting the income and loss items of the partnership and multiplying that amount by the highest tax rate (whether individual or corporate). No deduction is allowed for the amount of the imputed underpayment. Under either approach, partnership-level adjustments would not affect prior-year returns of any partners.

The following table sets forth various examination procedures available in a partnership setting.

Type of Partnership	Audit System		
	Deficiency Procedures	Entity-Level Procedures	Electing Large P/S Procedures
Small Partnership (No Pass-Through Partner)	X	X	
Small Partnership (Pass-Through Partner)		X	
More Than 10 Partners		X	
Over 100 Partners (Excluding Service Partners)		X	X

For electing large partnerships, information returns must be furnished to the partners by the first March 15 following the close of the partnership year. Furthermore, all partnerships with more than 100 partners must file Forms 1065 and the accompanying schedules (Forms K-1) on magnetic media. The electing large partnership provisions, as well as the return filing provisions, apply to partnership tax years ending on or after December 31, 1997.

Several significant changes or clarifications have been made to the manner in which various statutes of limitations operate in partnership cases:

❏ For settlements entered into after the date of enactment, the one-year partner-level statute of limitation on assessments for underpayments resulting from partnership-level adjustments does not begin to run until all such items are settled, even though some may have been subject to a prior settlement agreement.

❏ As is the case in non-entity level proceedings, refund claims relating to partnership or affected items may now be filed within the six month period following the expiration of any voluntary extension of the partnership statute of limitations. This change takes effect as if it were included in the original enactment of the entity-level audit rules enacted in 1982.

❏ Claims for refunds based on partnership-level deductions for bad debts or worthless securities may now be filed within seven years of the due date of the partnership return. This rule is effective as if it had been included in the original enactment of the entity-level audit rules in 1982.

❏ Even though a tax matters partner's authority terminates when the tax matters partner files for bankruptcy, any post-enactment consents signed by the tax matters partner after entering bankruptcy that extends the partnership statute of limitation will be considered valid, unless the IRS is actually notified of the bankruptcy proceeding.

❏ Any Tax Court petition, not only those timely filed, challenging a proposed partnership-level adjustment, will suspend the partner-level statute of limitations for assessment. In addition, if a bankruptcy petition is filed naming a partner as a debtor in a bankruptcy proceeding, the partner-level statute of limitations on the assessment and collection of tax pertaining to partnership-level adjustments is suspended for the period of time during which the IRS is prohibited from mailing an assessment and for 60 days thereafter. These amendments apply to partnership tax years that are still open on the date of enactment.

New procedures are available to partners to resolve adjustments proposed for a given year resulting from both partnership- and individual-level tax audits:

❏ A declaratory judgment procedure allows partners to challenge nonpartnership-level adjustments to their individual tax returns in Tax Court while awaiting the resolution of an entity-level proceeding. Alternatively, if a partner chooses to forego the declaratory judgment procedure, a refund claim may be filed at the conclusion of the partnership proceeding. This procedure will apply to partnership tax years ending after the date of enactment.

❏ Effective as if part of the original enactment of the entity-level audit rules in 1982, a procedure is now provided to allow a partner's spouse to raise the innocent spouse defense to any tax liability relating to a partnership-level adjustment in either a Tax Court petition or a refund suit.

❏ Actions by individual partners to enjoin premature assessments relating to partnership-level adjustments are now subject to Tax Court jurisdiction, as are petitions by individual partners challenging assessments of partnership-level adjustments on the ground that the partner-level statute of limitations has expired. These amendments are effective for partnership tax years ending after the date of enactment.

Finally, penalties related to partnership-level items are to be included in the entity-level proceeding for partnership tax years ending after the date of enactment, and interest on underpayments resulting from partnership-level adjustments is suspended if there is a delay in computing the partner-level effects of an entity-level settlement. Where appropriate, interest will be suspended with respect to adjustments for tax years beginning after the date of enactment.

Corporate Tax Shelter Registration

Under the new law, a "corporate tax shelter" must be registered with the Treasury Department by its promoter. If the promoter is a non-U.S. person, then, as a general rule, a U.S. participant is required to register the shelter.

A corporate tax shelter is any investment, plan, arrangement or transaction that (1) has as a significant purpose tax avoidance or evasion by a corporate participant, (2) is offered to any potential participant under conditions of confidentiality, and (3) may generate total fees in excess of $100,000 for its promoter.

Registration requires the submission of information identifying and describing the tax shelter and its tax benefits and other information the Treasury Department may require. In addition, promoters must maintain lists of those who have signed confidentiality agreements and those paying fees with respect to plans or arrangements that have previously been registered.

Corporate Tax Shelters

Summary of Requirements

❑ Register with the Treasury;
❑ Maintain list of participants who:
  - have signed confidentiality agreements
  - are paying fees with respect to plans that have previously been registered.

A failure to register may be penalized in an amount that is the greater of $10,000 or 50 percent of the fees payable to any promoter with respect to offerings prior to the date of late registration. A similar penalty applies to actual participants who were required to register the shelter but is limited to 50 percent of the fees the participant paid. Intentional disregard of the registration requirement increases the 50 percent penalty rate to 75 percent.

A Treasury report is due to Congress within one year of the enactment of the corporate tax shelter registration provision, addressing (1) enforcement efforts to enjoin promoters of abusive tax shelters, (2) the sufficiency of penalties applicable to corporate tax shelters, and (3) the need to extend the registration requirement to noncorporate investors.

The registration rules do not take effect until the IRS issues necessary guidance with respect to the filing requirements.

Estimated Taxes

The due date for first quarter estimated tax payments for a tax-exempt private foundation is moved to the fifteenth day of the fifth month of the tax year. This provision applies to tax years beginning after the date of enactment. See page 126.

The current $500 threshold for underpayments of tax taken into account in determining the applicability of individual estimated tax payment penalties is increased to $1,000 for tax years beginning after December 31, 1997. See page 23.

The current safe harbor provision requiring individuals with adjusted gross income in excess of $150,000 in the preceding tax year to pay 110 percent of that tax to avoid imposition of estimated tax payment penalties is modified. For tax years beginning in 1999, 2000 and 2001, the safe harbor will be met if 105 percent of the prior year's tax is paid via estimated tax payments; for tax years beginning in 2002 the safe harbor requirement will be 112 percent; and for tax years 2003 and thereafter the safe harbor will return to 110 percent.

Information Returns

The reporting threshold for payments for services made by federal executive agencies to any person, including a corporation, is reduced from $25,000 to $600 for returns due more than 90 days after the date of enactment. An exception is provided for certain classified or confidential contracts.

The requirement to report real estate sales is eliminated for sales of personal residences where the gross sales price does not exceed $500,000 ($250,000 in the case of a seller whose filing status is other than married filing jointly), provided the real estate reporting person obtains written assurances from the seller that (1) any gain will be exempt from tax, and (2) no seller financing was federally subsidized indebtedness. This amendment applies to sales or exchanges occurring after May 6, 1997.

Coopers & Lybrand L.L.P.

Unless reportable on Form 1099-MISC or Form W-2, any post-December 31, 1997, payment for legal services made to an attorney in the course of a trade or business must be reported on Form 1099-B, whether or not the attorney is the exclusive payee. In addition, payments made to corporations providing legal services are likewise reportable under Section 6041 (Form 1099-MISC) or Section 6045 (Form 1099-B).

Interest

Interest on underpayments reduced or eliminated by foreign tax credit carry-backs runs from the due date of the return of the underpayment year to the due date of the return for the year in which the foreign taxes subject to the carryback are actually paid or accrued. Also, for interest computation purposes, if a net operating loss or net capital loss carryback results in a foreign tax credit carryback, any proposed underpayment in an earlier year will not be considered as eliminated or reduced by the foreign tax credit carryback nor will an overpayment be considered as generated by the carryback until the due date of the loss-year return. These changes apply to foreign tax credit carrybacks arising in tax years beginning after the date of enactment.

For purposes of determining the date from which the increased interest rate on a large corporate underpayment of tax (the federal short-term rate plus five percentage points) applies, any letter or notice will be disregarded if the amount of the deficiency, proposed deficiency, assessment, or proposed assessment set forth in the letter or notice does not exceed $100,000 exclusive of interest, penalties or additions to tax. This rule applies to interest computations for periods after December 31, 1997.

Penalties

EFTPS Penalty Delay

Over 1.2 million businesses were originally required to begin making their tax deposits via EFTPS by January 1, 1997 (any business that deposited in excess of $50,000 of 1995 payroll taxes). This timeframe was extended to July 1, 1997, by the Small Business Job Protection Act of 1996. Furthermore, on June

2, 1997, the IRS announced that it would not impose penalties through December 31, 1997, on businesses for failure to make their deposits via EFTPS provided they made timely deposits using paper federal tax deposit coupons. In addition to those businesses required to begin using EFTPS in 1997, businesses that did not deposit payroll taxes in 1996 but deposited any other type of tax exceeding $50,000 during 1995 or 1996 are required to begin making electronic deposits in 1998. However, no penalties will be imposed against a tax depositor for failure to make electronic deposits before July 1, 1998, provided the depositor was not required to make electronic deposits before 1997.

EFTPS Deadline Changes

For businesses not required to make electronic payments before 1997:

❑ No penalties through June 30, 1998.

Substantial Understatement Penalty

The substantial understatement penalty is amended to conform the definition of the term "tax shelter" with that used for corporate tax shelter registration purposes. A further amendment provides that a corporation can never have a reasonable basis for an underpayment of tax and, therefore, avoid the assertion of a substantial underpayment penalty if the underpayment arises from its tax treatment of an item attributable to a multi-party financing transaction that does not clearly reflect income of the corporation. These amendments apply to transactions entered into after the date of enactment.

Reasonable Cause Exceptions

For tax years beginning after the date of enactment, the following penalties can now be waived if reasonable cause exists for the failure on which they are based:

❑ the penalty for failure to make a report in connection with deductible employee contributions to a retirement savings plan;

Coopers & Lybrand L.L.P.

- the penalty for failure to make a report as to certain small business stock;
- the penalty for failure of a foreign corporation to file a return of personal holding company tax; and
- the penalty for failure to make required payments for entities electing not to have the required tax year.

Returns

A beneficiary of an estate or trust is required to file its return in a manner that is consistent with the information return (generally Schedule K-1) received from the estate or trust, unless a notification of inconsistency is filed with the beneficiary's return. This rule applies to returns filed after the date of enactment.

Statutes of Limitation

Refund claims filed within three years of the return due date but after the issuance of a deficiency notice will be considered valid, even if a tax return has not been filed. This change applies to refund claims for tax years ending after the date of enactment.

The running of the statute of limitations for assessments of underpayments attributable to distributions from a third party commences with the filing date of the return of the recipient of the distribution (e.g., S corporation shareholder) and not that of the third-party's tax return. This change applies to tax years ending after the date of enactment.

Tax Court

Clarification is provided confirming that Tax Court ordered refunds of tax and interest are appealable in the same manner as other Tax Court decisions. However, the Tax Court's jurisdiction is not extended to consideration of the merits of any credits or offset (e.g., liability for student loans, child support, etc.), which reduces or eliminates the payment of any refund.

Tax Court jurisdiction is extended to cases involving IRS determinations that service providers are employees rather than independent contractors and that relief from such reclassifications is not available under Section 530 of the

Revenue Act of 1978. Any decision of the Tax Court is reviewable by the appropriate United States Court of Appeals.

Any challenge to an IRS interest calculation related to a Tax Court decision must be filed in the form of a "Motion" rather than a "Petition."

All changes to Tax Court procedure take effect upon the date of enactment.

Payments

The IRS is authorized to accept payments of tax by any commercially acceptable means, including electronic funds transfers, such as those arising from credit cards, debit cards and charge cards. This provision will take effect nine months after the date of enactment.

Employment Taxes

Securities Brokers

The fact that the organization for which a securities broker renders services is required to provide certain instructions to such a worker to comply with governmental investor protection standards or investor protection standards imposed by a governing body pursuant to delegation by a federal or state agency is to be disregarded when considering the worker's proper classification for employment tax purposes. This rule applies to services performed after December 31, 1997.

Self Employment Contribution Act (SECA) Taxes

Recent cases have held that certain payments received by former insurance salesmen are not subject to SECA taxes. These holdings are now codified. Payments received from an insurance company for prior services performed as an insurance salesman will not be subject to SECA tax provided:

❑ the amounts are received after termination of the individual's relationship with the company;

❏ no services are performed after termination and before the tax year-end;

❏ the amounts relate solely to policies that are sold during the last year of the relationship but remain effective after termination; and

❏ the payments are conditioned on a noncompete arrangement for at least one year following termination.

This rule applies to payments made after December 31, 1997.

Tax-Exempt Organizations

Unrelated Business Income Exclusion

The new law will exempt "corporate sponsorship" payments from the unrelated business income tax (UBIT). This provision follows the proposed Treasury regulations in this area, which generally exempt from tax any payment where the corporate sponsor receives an acknowledgement from the exempt organization of its name or its commonly known logo. Current proposed regulations, however, would tax payments received for product advertising.

Under the new law, payments from a sponsor for both advertising and sponsor acknowledgement will not be subject to tax for the amount in excess of the fair market value of the advertising provided. The new law also states that the sponsorship exclusion does not apply to periodicals or qualified conventions and trade shows.

These rules apply to payments solicited or paid after December 31, 1997.

Controlled Subsidiaries

Generally, interest, royalties and rental income from real property are excluded from the tax of a tax-exempt organization. However, prior law overrides this normal exclusion of interest, rents and royalties paid from an 80 percent directly controlled subsidiary. Organizations were avoiding this provision by tiering subsidiaries, or by holding 79 percent of the controlled subsidiary, and then had the interest, rents and royalties paid from the lower-tier group. The new law expands the rules and changes the control factor to a 50-percent direct or indirect control of the payee organization, which restricts this planning opportunity.

The new law is effective for tax years beginning after the date of enactment. A delayed two-year transition applies for transactions with a binding contract on June 8, 1997.

Cap On Qualified Bonds

The $150 million limit on qualified Section 501(c)(3) bonds is lifted for bonds issued solely for capital expenditures incurred after the date of enactment.

Estimated Taxes of Private Foundations

The new law changes the due date for the first estimated tax payment for investment income from April 15 to May 15, the due date of a calendar-year organization's information return, Form 990-PF. The new due date is effective for tax years beginning after the date of enactment.

Contributions of Appreciated Stock to Private Foundations

The new law extends the provision that allows donors to take a full deduction, not merely basis, for a gift of appreciated stock, where market quotations are readily available, to a private foundation. The extension expires for gifts made after June 30, 1998.

Proxy Tax Requirements and Reporting

The new law provides an exemption from the general disclosure requirements and proxy tax (a tax on lobbying and political activities of an organization where members were not informed that a portion of their dues was not deductible) and where 90 percent of the aggregate annual dues (or similar payments) are paid by tax exempt entities, individuals or families whose annual dues are less than $100 (indexed). The effective date is December 31, 1997.

Charitable Deduction for Mileage Raised

The charitable deduction for mileage was raised from 12 cents per mile to 14 cents per mile effective for tax years beginning in 1998. This amount is not indexed for inflation.

Excise Taxes

Air Transportation

The excise taxes on transportation of persons and property are extended from September 30, 1997 to September 30, 2007. Significant changes are made to the rates and application of this excise tax to taxable transportation of persons (the so-called "ticket tax"). It continues at its current rate of 10 percent through September 30, 1997 and is gradually reduced to 7.5 percent by October 1, 1999. However, any taxable air transportation beginning or ending at a rural airport is subject to the 7.5 percent rate effective October 1, 1997.

An additional tax is imposed on each domestic segment of taxable transportation by air. Beginning October 1, 1997 the tax is set at $1.00 and periodically increases until it reaches $3.00 on January 1, 2002 after which date it will be adjusted for inflation. A "domestic segment" is taxable transportation consisting of one takeoff and one landing but does not include either takeoffs from, or landings at, rural airports.

Passengers arriving from, or departing for, other countries are subject to a $12.00 tax on any amounts paid for air transportation. To the extent this tax would apply to a domestic segment beginning or ending in Alaska or Hawaii, it only applies to departures at a rate of $6.00. Both rates are subject to adjustments for inflation after 1998.

The excise tax on taxable air transportation is extended to amounts paid to air carriers (in cash or in kind) for the right to award or otherwise distribute free or reduced-rate air transportation. Such amounts include payments for frequent flyer miles purchased by credit card companies, telephone companies, and rental car companies for distribution to customers and others.

These amendments apply to transportation beginning on or after October 1, 1997, unless the ticket is for transportation to or from a foreign country and was paid for before the date of enactment. The extension of the excise tax to amounts paid for the right to provide mileage awards only applies to amounts paid after September 30, 1997, unless there were prior payments between members of a controlled group.

Communications

Amounts paid (in cash or in kind) for the right to award or otherwise distribute free or reduced-rate long-distance telephone service are subject to the three-percent excise tax on communications services. This tax applies to such payments as those made for prepaid telephone cards offered through service stations and convenience stores and is effective for amounts paid in calendar months beginning more than 60 days after the date of enactment.

Distilled Spirits, Wine, and Beer

Changes made to the excise tax provisions pertaining to distilled spirits, wine, and beer would allow, in part, for:

❑ refunds or credits of tax on imported bottled spirits returned to distilled spirit plants,

❑ refunds or credits of tax on domestic wine returned to bond, and

❑ exemptions from tax for beer withdrawn from customs bonded warehouses for embassy use as well as for domestic beer withdrawn from a brewery for destruction.

All changes to the excise tax provisions relating to distilled spirits, wine, and beer take effect the first day of the first calendar quarter that begins at least 180 days after date of enactment.

Environmental

The Leaking Underground Storage Tank (LUST) Trust Fund excise tax of 0.1 cent per gallon on gasoline, diesel fuel, special motor fuels (other than liquefied petroleum gas), aviation fuels, and inland waterways fuels is reinstated for the period October 1, 1997 to March 31, 2005.

Effective as of the date of enactment, the excise tax on ozone depleting chemicals has been extended to imported recycled halon-1211.

Cigarettes and Tobacco

Under prior law, the current federal excise tax on cigarettes is 24 cents per pack. Various rates of tax are also levied against other tobacco products.

The new law increases the cigarette tax by 10 cents per pack in 2000, and an additional 5 cents per pack in 2002. The new law also provides a proportionate increase in other tobacco products' excise tax.

Other Changes

Additional excise tax changes made by the new law affect the following items:

- ❑ kerosene
- ❑ motor fuels
- ❑ diesel fuels
- ❑ aviator fuel refund
- ❑ skydiving flights
- ❑ post-purchase parts and accessories additions
- ❑ wrecked vehicles
- ❑ tires
- ❑ highway trucks and trailers
- ❑ registration for tax-free sales
- ❑ arrows
- ❑ vaccine

Pensions

Diversification of Section 401(k) Investments

The new law limits the extent to which a company can mandate that employees invest their contributions to Section 401(k) plans in company stock. Under the new law, the amount of elective deferrals to a Section 401(k) plan required to be invested in "qualifying employer securities" or "qualifying employer real property" will be limited to 10 percent of total deferrals and earnings for plan years beginning after 1998.

Three categories of plans, however, will not be subject to this constraint. These categories include ESOPs as well as individual account plans with assets that do not equal or exceed 10 percent of the fair market value of all pension plan assets of the employer. Individual account plans also will escape this rule if elective deferrals required to be invested in employer stock or real property do not exceed more than one percent of an employee's compensation.

> **Observation:** Most employers should find that their plans will not be constrained by these limits. Plans that permit all elective deferrals to be invested at the discretion of the participant will, of course, not be subject to these new rules. Further, the new rules place no limits on the investment of employer-matching contributions in employer stock.

Excess Distribution Tax

The 15-percent excess distribution tax has been repealed for distributions received after 1996. The 15-percent excise tax on certain retirement accumulations in an individual's estate has also been eliminated for persons dying after 1996.

> Observation: As a result of this change, tax and estate planning will no longer need to focus on the timing and form of distributions to avoid these excise taxes. The advantages of leaving retirement money in a qualified plan or individual retirement account to reap the benefits of tax deferral will continue to play a significant role in tax planning. The lowering of the capital gains rate, however, will inject a new element into this decision-making process.

The 10-percent excise tax on contributions that are nondeductible because they exceed a special deduction limit that applies when a company sponsors both a defined benefit and a defined contribution plan is modified. In a prior tax law change, the excise tax was waived for contributions to a defined contribution plan—up to a limit of 6 percent of compensation—if the contributions were not deductible because they exceeded the special limit. The new rules expand this waiver so that an employer may generally contribute the sum of matching contributions and Section 401(k) elective deferrals to a plan for a year without incurring the excise tax. No change was made, however, to the deduction limits. This provision is effective for tax years beginning after December 31, 1997.

Lump-Sum Cashouts

Plans will be permitted to cash out employees with lump sums of $5,000 or less, starting with plan years beginning after the date of enactment.

> Observation: This increase in the lump sum limit will provide a great deal of administrative (and some monetary) relief for employers that have had to maintain records, provide reports, pay PBGC premiums, etc., over the years for employees with small accrued benefits. Employers that have

no cashout provision in their plans at present may wish to consider implementing such a provision. Employers with plans that reflect the $3,500 limit may want to amend their plans to increase the limit.

Government Plans

Most of the qualification rules are made inapplicable to government plans; the list includes the nondiscrimination rules, the participation rules and the testing rules for Section 401(k) plans. Government plans will also escape the nondiscrimination rules applicable to Section 403(b) plans—the rules with respect to the availability of salary reduction agreements will remain in force. A government plan will be considered to have satisfied all of these rules for years before the new law. This provision is effective for tax years beginning on or after the date of enactment.

Miscellaneous

❑ The current full-funding limit of 150 percent of current liability is increased to 155 percent for plan years beginning in 1999 and 2000; 160 percent for 2001 and 2002; 165 percent for 2003 and 2004; and 170 percent for 2005 and thereafter. The related amortization requirements are changed so that a plan will amortize, over 20 years (instead of the current 10), the contributions that would have been required to be made to the plan were it not for the full funding limit.

❑ The first-level tax imposed on prohibited transactions is increased from 10 percent to 15 percent for prohibited transactions occurring after the date of enactment.

❑ An additional simplified table is provided for use after 1997 in determining the taxable portion of a person's annuity payments. The table in prior law will continue to be used for taxpayers receiving a single-life annuity. The new table added by the new law will provide a second table for use by persons receiving benefits based on the lives of more than one annuitant.

❏ The new rules provide that matching contributions made on behalf of self-employed individuals will not be treated as elective deferrals by these individuals and, thus, will not be subject to the $9,500 limit on elective deferrals. Comparable treatment will be accorded matching contributions to a self-employed individual in a SIMPLE IRA account. These changes will be effective in 1998 for Section 401(k) plans and in 1997 for SIMPLE IRAs.

❏ New regulations will be issued to clarify that with respect to whether a rollover from one plan to another is a valid rollover (and one that will not disqualify the accepting plan), it is not necessary for the plan that originates the rollover to have a determination letter. The change is to be effective for rollover contributions made after 1997.

❏ The new rules significantly expand the circumstances under which a person's qualified plan benefit may be offset to repay the amount owed by the individual on account of a breach of fiduciary duty or crime involving the plan. The change will be effective for judgments and other orders issued after the date of enactment.

❏ Effective with enactment, the new rules eliminate the requirement that summary plan descriptions and summaries of material modifications be filed with the DOL, although the department will still have the right to receive them upon request.

❏ The new rules require guidance to be issued by the end of 1998 regarding the extent to which plans may use "new technologies" to fulfill notice, election, consent, disclosure and time requirements as well as related record-keeping requirements. Guidance is also required to clarify the extent to which pension-related "writing requirements" may be satisfied by paperless transactions.

❏ The manner in which the exclusion allowance under Section 403(b) is calculated is revised to provide that, after 1997, "includible compensation" will include elective deferrals and amounts contributed to a cafeteria plan or a Section 457 plan that are not includible in income. The new rules also adjust the alternate Section 415 limit on the exclusion allowance by directing Section 403(b) regulations to be modified to reflect the repeal of the Section 415(e) combined limit after 1999. This modification is to be effective for years beginning after 1999.

❑ The new rules amend the maximum contribution limits under Section 415(b)(2) to provide special limits after 1997 for contributions made by an employee to purchase service credit in a government plan.

❑ For tax years after 1997, the new rules amend Section 409(h) to permit an ESOP of an S corporation to make distributions in cash as well as in employer securities, provided the employee has the right to require the employer to purchase the securities. The exception also is extended to certain prohibited transaction rules to shareholder employees of S corporations.

❑ For transfers made from the trusts to ESOPs after the date of enactment, the new rules permit, under certain circumstances, the transfer of a remainder interest of qualified employer securities from a charitable remainder trust to an ESOP.

❑ There are a number of small changes to SIMPLE plans. Among others, the new rules permit an employer to sponsor a SIMPLE plan even though the employer also sponsors a qualified plan for union employees, provided the union employees are not permitted to participate in the SIMPLE plan.

Appendices

Estimated Budget Effect of Major Provisions (1997–2007)

Individual Tax Liability Comparison

Comparison of New Law to Prior Law

Appendix A

Estimated Budget Effect of Major Provisions (1997–2007)
(in millions of dollars)

Provision	1997	1998	1999	2000	2001	2002	1997–2002	1997–2007
Individual Tax Provisions								
Child Tax Credit	—	-2,710	-18,119	-21,549	-21,401	-21,258	-85,037	-183,384
Education Tax Incentives	—	-2,966	-7,983	-9,178	-9,672	-9,595	-39,394	-98,835
Expanded IRAs	—	-367	-345	86	-346	-860	-1,832	-20,225
Capital Gains Rate and Home Sale Exclusion	1,254	6,371	171	-2,954	-2,934	-1,785	123	-21,161
Estate and Gift Tax	—	-33	-922	-1,341	-1,919	-2,139	-6,354	-34,450
Business Tax Provisions								
Alternative Minimum Tax	-8	-254	-909	-1,951	-2,494	-2,592	-8,209	-19,951
District of Columbia Tax Incentives	—	-82	-136	-152	-155	-160	-686	-1,158
Research Credit	-161	-820	-639	-294	-204	-123	-2,241	-2,274
Health Insurance Deduction for Self Employed	—	—	—	-39	-120	-224	-383	-3,479
Foreign Tax Provisions	—	-95	-179	-244	-289	-313	-1,122	-4,102

Coopers & Lybrand L.L.P.

Revenue Increases

Airport Trust Fund Excise Taxes and International Arrival and Departure Taxes	-1,017	5,649	7,434	6,496	7,014	7,580	33,157	79,691
Extend FUTA surtax through 2007	—	—	1,063	1,763	1,797	1,733	6,356	6,726
Cigarettes/tobacco excise taxes*	—	—	–	1,175	1,720	2,272	5,167	16,667
Short-against-the-box and other financial products provisions	—	463	439	480	460	442	2,284	3,811
"Morris Trust" corporate reorganization transactions	—	301	243	216	187	158	1,105	1,465
Levy exemption	—	332	327	256	213	157	1,285	1,750
NOL carryover	—	42	303	361	256	179	1,141	1,672
Miscellaneous Provisions	-8	-15,311	9,365	107	278	4,935	-636	1,859
Net Tax Cuts	60	-9,480	-9,887	-26,762	-27,609	-21,593	-95,276	-275,378

* Cigarette/tobacco excise increase was enacted as part of H.R. 2015, "The Balanced Budget Act of 1997."

Analysis: 1997 Tax Legislation

Appendix B

Individual Tax Liability Comparison

Families With Two Children

1998 AGI	$25,000	$50,000	$80,000	$150,000	$600,000
Wages and other income	$24,750	$49,250	$78,000	$142,500	$510,000
Capital gain income	250	750	2,000	7,500	90,000
Adjusted gross income *(a)*	25,000	50,000	80,000	150,000	600,000
Exemptions	(10,800)	(10,800)	(10,800)	(10,800)	N/A
Deductions	(8,644)	(11,290)	(16,692)	(28,735) *(d)*	(60,628)
Taxable income	5,556	27,910	52,508	110,465	539,372
Tax Computation					
1998 prior law: *(c)*					
Ordinary	795	4,074	8,630	23,351	151,510
Capital	38	113	400	2,100	25,200
Total prior law tax	**833**	**4,187**	**9,030**	**25,451**	**176,710**

1998 new law:					
Taxable income	5,556	27,910	52,508	110,465	539,372
Deductible IRA contribution (a)	(4,000)	(4,000)	(2,000)	(2,000)	N/A
New taxable income	1,556	23,910	50,508	108,465	539,372
Ordinary	196	3,474	8,247	22,778	151,510
Capital	25	75	400	1,500	18,000
Tax before credits	221	3,549	8,647	24,278	169,510
Child credit	(400) (b)	(400)	(400)	N/A	N/A
Education credit	(1,500) (e)	(1,500)	(1,500)	N/A	N/A
Earned income tax credit	(1,134)	N/A	N/A	N/A	N/A
Total new law tax	**(913)**	**1,649**	**6,747**	**24,278**	**169,510**
Savings	**$1,746**	**$2,538**	**$2,283**	**$1,173**	**$7,200**
	210%	61%	25%	5%	4%

(a) Qualifying IRA contributions are actually deducted before arriving at an individual's adjusted gross income. (Phased-out for higher income individuals.)
(b) Child credit can only be refundable with families comprised of three or more children.
(c) Taxpayer does not qualify for IRA contribution provisions.
(d) The allowable deductions under prior law would actually be reduced by $60 because no deductible IRA contribution would be available.
(e) Hope education credits are not refundable.
N/A = not available due to phase-out for higher-income individuals.

Assumptions

Each family consists of a married couple filing a joint tax return with their two children, one in the first year of college (with $5,000 of qualified education expenses), the other child is under age 13. The couple makes the maximum deductible IRA contribution where one of the spouses is not a participant in a qualified retirement plan. The tax rates and exemption amounts are indexed for inflation as under current law, with the new $400 child credit and $1,500 Hope Scholarship credit analyzed. Capital gain income and itemized deductions are based on averages obtained from IRS data. Capital assets sold were held for at least eighteen months.

Appendix C

Individuals

Selected Provisions From Analysis: 1997 Tax Legislation

Page	Subject	Prior Law	1997 Tax Act	Effective Date	Revenue Over 5 Years
8	Child Credit	No provision.	$500 tax credit for children under age 17 ($400 in 1998); phaseout begins at $75,000 (single)/$110,000 (joint) modified AGI.	1/1/98	-$85 billion
12	"HOPE" Tax Credit	No provision.	$1,500 credit for first two years of higher education expenses; phaseout complete at $50,000 (single)/ $100,000 (joint) modified AGI.	Expenses paid after 12/31/97 for education furnished after that date.	-$31.5 billion (and Lifetime Credit)
12	Lifetime Learning Tax Credit	No provision.	Credit of 20% of $5,000 ($10,000 for tax years beginning in 2003) of qualified education, phaseout complete at $50,000 (single)/ $100,000 (joint) modified AGI.	Expenses paid after 6/30/98 for education furnished after that date.	(See above.)
15	Qualified Prepaid State Tuition Programs	Qualified higher education expenses do not include room and board.	Room and board are qualified expenses.	Tax years after 8/20/96.	-$534 million

144

Page	Subject	Prior Law	1997 Tax Act	Effective Date	Revenue Over 5 Years
15	Education IRA	No provision.	Distributions for post-secondary education expenses excluded from income; contributions nondeductible and limited to $500.	1/1/98	-$3.9 billion
16	Student Loan Interest Deduction	Student loan interest is nondeductible personal interest.	Above-the-line deduction for qualified interest; phaseout begins at $40,000 (single)/$60,000 (joint).	Interest payments due after 12/31/97.	-$690 million
17	IRA Education Withdrawals	Amounts withdrawn prior to age 59 1/2 subject to 10% early withdrawal penalty.	No penalty on amounts withdrawn for higher education of self, spouse, child or grandchild.	Withdrawals after 12/31/97 for expenses paid and education furnished after that date.	-$812 million
17	Employer-Provided Education Assistance	$5,250 exclusion for employer assistance for undergraduate courses beginning before 6/30/97.	Undergraduate exclusion extended through 5/31/00.	Tax years beginning after 12/31/96.	-$1.15 billion

Page	Subject	Prior Law	1997 Tax Act	Effective Date	Revenue Over 5 Years
18	IRA Contributions	$2,000 deduction for IRA contributions if individual or spouse is active participant; phase-out begins at $25,000 (single)/$40,000 (joint).	Phaseout begins at $30,000 (single)/$50,000 (joint) in 1998; $150,000/$160,000 for non-active spouses.	Tax years beginning after 12/31/97.	-$1.8 billion (and withdrawals, penalties, distributions)
21	IRA Withdrawals	Withdrawals prior to age 59 1/2 subject to 10% early withdrawal penalty.	Penalty-free withdrawals for education and first-time home expenses.	Tax years beginning after 12/31/97.	(See above.)
21	Roth IRAs	No provision.	Qualified distributions (first home purchase, death) excluded from income; no penalty applies.	Tax years beginning after 12/31/97.	(See above.)
22	Standard Deduction for Dependents	Child's standard deduction is lesser of individual deduction or greater of $500 or earned income.	Add $250 to earned income to calculate deduction.	1/1/98	-$145 million (includes AMT)

Page	Subject	Prior Law	1997 Tax Act	Effective Date	Revenue Over 5 Years
22	Child AMT Exemption	AMT exemption is lesser of single AMT exemption of $33,750 or $1,400 plus earned income.	Exemption lesser of $33,750 or sum of child's earned income plus $5,000.	1/1/98	(See above.)
23	Estimated Taxes	Estimated tax requirements and penalties apply to tax over $500.	Increased to $1,000.	Tax years beginning after 12/31/97.	-$208 million
25	Individual Capital Gains	28% maximum rate.	20% maximum rate for assets held more than 18 months; new 10% rate applies to gain currently taxable at 15%; 18%/8% rates for assets held over 5 years starting in 2001; 28% maximum rate for "mid-term gain" assets and collectibles; 25% maximum on Section 1250 recapture.	Sales or exchanges on or after 5/7/97.	$123 million (with sale of principal residence and QSBS rollover provisions)

Page	Subject	Prior Law	1997 Tax Act	Effective Date	Revenue Over 5 Years
31	Sale of Principal Residence	Nonrecognition of gain on sale of principal residence if new residence cost equals sale price of former residence; one-time $125,000 exclusion for age 55 and over.	$250,000 ($500,000 joint) gain on sale of residence excluded if qualifies as principal residence for two of five preceding years; one-time exclusion repealed.	Sales of principal residences after 5/6/97.	(See above.)
32	Qualified Small Business Stock (QSBS) Rollover	Individuals may exclude 50% of gain on sale of qualified small business stock; 50% minimum tax preference on excluded gain.	Individual may rollover gain on sale of QSBS held more than 6 months if proceeds used to purchase other QSBS within 60 days; 42% tax preference on excluded gain.	Sales after date of enactment.	(See above.)
33	Short-Against-The-Box Transactions	No gain or loss recognized on certain transactions designed to eliminate risk of loss.	Gain recognition on constructive sales of any appreciated financial position in stock, partnership or certain debt instruments.	Constructive sales entered into after 6/8/97.	$708 million

Business

Page	Subject	Prior Law	1997 Tax Act	Effective Date	Revenue Over 5 Years
34	Mark-to-Market Accounting	Securities dealers must use mark-to-market rules.	Securities traders and commodities dealers and traders may elect mark-to-market.	Tax years ending after date of enactment.	Not available.
37	Net Operating Losses	3-year carryback and 15-year carryforward of NOLs; may elect to forego 3-year carryback.	2-year carryback and 20-year carryforward; does not apply to NOLs carried forward from tax years beginning before effective date.	NOLs generated in tax years beginning after date of enactment.	$1.1 billion
38	General Business Credits	3-year carryback and 15-year carryforward.	1-year carryback and 20-year carryforward.	Credits arising in tax years beginning after 12/31/97.	$471 million
39	Alternative Minimum Tax Depreciation Adjustment	Regular tax depreciation uses shorter recovery periods for tangible personal property than AMT.	Conforms AMT depreciation lives to regular tax lives of property.	For tangible property placed in service after 12/31/98.	-$6.8 billion
40	Small Corporation AMT	Minimum tax is 20% of AMT income over a phased-out $40,000 exemption.	Repeals corporate AMT for small corporations; minimum tax credit limited to corporation's regular tax liability over 25% of its regular tax in excess of $25,000.	Tax years beginning after 12/31/97.	-$577 million

Page	Subject	Prior Law	1997 Tax Act	Effective Date	Revenue Over 5 Years
41	Corporate-Owned Life Insurance Premium Deduction Limitation	No deduction for premiums paid on life of officer, employee or financially interested person when corporation is policy beneficiary.	No deduction for premiums on endowment and annuity contracts if taxpayer is direct beneficiary, regardless of insured.	Contracts issued after 6/8/97.	$500 million (with interest deduction, debt to fund, life insurance company and contract lapse)
42	COLI Interest Deduction Limitation	No deduction for interest on debt incurred to buy or carry tax-exempt obligations; proceeds from contract sales in excess of basis taxable.	Extends life insurance interest deduction limitations to all individuals; limits its unrelated interest to business life insurance purchase.	Contracts issued after 6/8/97.	(See above.)
42	Debt to Fund Life Insurance	No provision.	Interest expense allocable on ratio of average unborrowed policy cash values of life insurance policies and annuity and endowment contracts to the average adjusted bases for all assets.	Contracts issued after 6/8/97.	(See above.)

Coopers & Lybrand L.L.P.

Page	Subject	Prior Law	1997 Tax Act	Effective Date	Revenue Over 5 Years
43	Insurance Purchased by Insurance Companies	No provision.	Increase in policy cash value treated as tax-exempt interest or dividend received deduction.	Contracts issued after 6/8/97.	(See above.)
44	Welfare-to-Work Tax Credit	No provision.	Wage credit of 35% of first $10,000, and 50% on $10,000 of wages in second year of employment for hires made through 4/30/99.	Wages paid or incurred for new hires beginning work after 12/31/97.	-$99 million
45	Corporate Contributions of Computer Technology	No provision.	Qualified contributions include gifts of computer technology and equipment made to certain institutions within 2 years after acquisition.	Tax years beginning after 1997 and before 1/1/00.	-$225 million
46	Dividends-Received Deduction (DRD)	DRD for corporate shareholder if 46-day holding period for dividend paying stock and 91-day period for certain preferred stock met.	DRD for dividend paying stock held over 45 days during 90-day period or preferred stock held 90 of 180 days.	Dividends received or accrued after 30 days after date of enactment.	$71 million

Page	Subject	Prior Law	1997 Tax Act	Effective Date	Revenue Over 5 Years
46	Pooled Debt Obligations- Credit Card Receivables	If principal may be paid without interest by specified date, holder need not accrue interest until after that date.	Holder must accrue interest or original issue discount based on reasonable assumption on timing of payments of accounts in pool.	Tax years beginning after date of enactment.	$1.3 billion
47	Interest Deductions on Certain Debt Instruments	Issuer of debt instrument with original issue discount (OID) accrues and deducts discount as interest over instrument's life.	No deduction for interest or OID on instrument issued by corporation that is payable in issuer or related party stock or convertible into stock at issuer's option.	Instruments issued after 6/8/97.	$148 million
49	Home Office Deduction	Portion of home must be principal place of business.	Definition expanded to include area exclusively used to conduct administrative or management activities if no other fixed location is used.	Tax years beginning after 12/31/98.	-$880 million

Coopers & Lybrand L.L.P.

Page	Subject	Prior Law	1997 Tax Act	Effective Date	Revenue Over 5 Years
50	Health Insurance for Self-Employed Individuals	Deductible health insurance percentage scheduled to increase to 80% by 2006.	Deductions increase from 40% in 1997 to 100% by 2007.	Tax years beginning after 12/31/96.	-$383 million
51	Research and Development Credit	20% credit until 5/31/97.	Credit extended 6/1/97 to 6/30/98.	6/1/97	-$2.2 billion
51	Contributions of Appreciated Stock	Deduct FMV of qualified appreciated stock contributed to private foundations through 5/31/97.	Extended 6/1/97 to 6/30/98.	6/1/97	-$112 million
51	Work Opportunity Tax Credit	35% WOTC credit to employers hiring targeted individuals through 9/30/97.	Credit extended 10/1/97 to 6/30/98; increased to 40%.	Wages paid or incurred for hires after 9/30/97.	-$383 million

Page	Subject	Prior Law	1997 Tax Act	Effective Date	Revenue Over 5 Years
51	Orphan Drug Tax Credit	50% tax credit for qualified clinical testing of orphan drugs through 5/31/97.	Permanently extended.	6/1/97	-$152 million
51	Employer-Provided Education Assistance	Excludes up to $5,250 of higher education costs through 6/30/97.	Extended 7/1/97 to 5/31/00.	Tax years beginning after 12/31/96.	-$1.2 billion
52	Inventory Shrinkage	No provision.	Inventory method does not fail to clearly reflect income solely because it estimates shrinkage.	Tax years ending after date of enactment.	-$103 million
54	Retail Tenant Allowances	Allowance to tenant is income if landlord does not own improvements or construction.	Allowance excluded if for leased property construction or improvement and does not exceed expenditure.	Leases entered into after date of enactment.	—
55	FUTA Excise Tax	Temporary surtax of 0.2% of taxable wages added to FUTA through 12/31/98.	Extend surtax through 12/31/07.	Labor performed on or after 1/1/99.	$6.4 billion

Page	Subject	Prior Law	1997 Tax Act	Effective Date	Revenue Over 5 Years
57	Tax-Exempt Bonds	If government bond proceeds spent within six months of issuance, no rebate of profits on unrelated business purpose investments; all but lessor of 5% of proceeds or $100,000 spent in six months, remainder within one year.	Repeals $100,000 limitation; rebate no longer applies to certain construction issues.	Bonds issued after date of enactment.	-$17 million
57	Private Activity Bonds	150% of debt service for bond year can be invested at a materially higher yield.	150% debt service-based limitation repealed.	Bonds issued after date of enactment.	—
59	Corporate Spin-offs and Morris Trust Transactions	No provision.	Certain post-spin-off acquisitions result in gain to distributing corporation.	Distributions after 4/16/97, except certain written binding contracts.	$1.105 billion (including meaning of control, intra-group spins)
61	Distributions of Controlled Corporate Stock	"Control" immediately after the distribution means at least 80% of voting power and 80% of each other stock class.	"Control" means at least 50% of vote and value of stock.	Transfers after date of enactment, except certain written binding contracts.	(See above.)

Page	Subject	Prior Law	1997 Tax Act	Effective Date	Revenue Over 5 Years
61	Intragroup Spin-offs	No provision.	Certain intragroup spin-offs that are part of Morris Trust transactions result in gain.	Intragroup distributions after 4/16/97, except certain written binding contracts.	(See above.)
62	Preferred Stock	Shareholders receive preferred stock tax-free in exchange for contributed property, or as part of corporate reorganization.	Receipt of certain nonqualified preferred stock is taxable.	Transactions after 6/8/97, except certain written binding contracts.	$194 million
63	Extraordinary Dividends	Extraordinary dividends reduce shareholder's stock basis if not taxed; excess amounts are gain upon subsequent sale.	Excess amounts are recognized as income immediately; dividends through option attribution treated as extraordinary dividends.	Distributions after 5/3/95, except certain written binding contracts and other exceptions.	-$103 million
64	Dividends in Reorganizations	Dividends received in a reorganization are treated under regular dividend rules.	Certain dividends treated as extraordinary dividends.	Distributions after 5/3/95, except certain written binding contracts and other exceptions.	(See above.)

Page	Subject	Prior Law	1997 Tax Act	Effective Date	Revenue Over 5 Years
65	Sale of Stock Between Related Corporations	Untaxed dividends do not reduce stock basis.	Untaxed dividends reduce stock basis.	Distributions or acquisitions after 6/8/97, except certain written binding contracts.	$35 million (including dividends)
66	Property Transfers to Investment Companies	Transfers do not qualify for nonrecognition treatment if company holds more than 80% of certain investment assets.	Expands types of investment assets considered for the 80% test.	Transfers after 6/8/97, except certain written binding contracts.	—
69	Estate and Gift Unified Credit Equivalent	$600,000 exempt from tax.	Increased to 1 million by 2006.	Deaths and gifts after 12/31/97.	-$5.9 million (with family-owned business exclusion and inflation indexing)
70	Family-owned Business Exclusion	No provision.	$1.3 million exclusion for family-owned business interests comprising over 50% of estate.	Deaths and gifts after 12/31/97.	(See above.)

Page	Subject	Prior Law	1997 Tax Act	Effective Date	Revenue Over 5 Years
71	Installment Payments of Closely Held Estate Tax	Estate tax on closely held interest payable over 14 years; interest-only payments for 4 years; 4% interest on first taxable $1 million.	Interest-only payments for 4 years; 2% interest on first taxable $1 million (indexed for inflation) with the remainder taxed at 45% of the underpayment penalty rate; interest nondeductible.	Deaths after 12/31/97; election for deaths before 1/1/98.	-$84 million
72	Charitable Remainder Annuity Trusts and Unitrusts	No provision.	50% annual payout cap; 10% minimum remainder interest.	Transfers to trust after 7/28/97.	$30 million
74	Generation-Skipping Tax Pre-Deceased Parent Exception	Tax waived on transfers from grandparent to grandchild when parent-predeceased; transfers to grandchildren from grandparent-funded trusts and from grandparent to siblings' grandchildren taxed.	Extends exception to transfers from grandparent-funded trusts and collateral heirs.	Transfers, terminations and distributions after 12/31/97.	-$16 million

Coopers & Lybrand L.L.P.

Page	Subject	Prior Law	1997 Tax Act	Effective Date	Revenue Over 5 Years
76	QTIP Right of Recovery	General language waives right to recover estate tax.	Specific language required.	Deaths after date of enactment.	—
77	Throwback Rules	Distributions from domestic trusts subject to throwback rules; property sold within 2 years of contribution taxed at contributor's marginal rate.	Most domestic trusts exempt; 2-year rule repealed for domestic and foreign trusts.	Distributions after date of enactment.	-$44 million
79	Foreign Sales Corporation (FSC) Benefits	Computer software not eligible for FSC benefits unless not reproduced for sale.	Computer software eligible and broadly defined.	Gross receipts in years ending after 12/31/97.	$568 million
81	Foreign Tax Credit	Creditable foreign income taxes are translated to U.S. dollars when tax paid.	Translation occurs at the average rate for the tax year.	Taxes paid or accrued in tax years beginning after 12/31/97.	<-$5 million
81	Deemed Paid Foreign Tax Credit	Credit not available for taxes paid below the third-tier.	Credit available for taxes paid by certain 4th-, 5th-, and 6th-tier foreign entities.	Taxes paid or accrued after date of enactment.	<-$2.5 million
82	Foreign Tax Credit Holding Period	Foreign tax credit allowed regardless of time foreign corporation stock held.	Imposes holding period requirement for claiming credit.	Dividends paid or accrued 30 days after date of enactment.	$230 million

Page	Subject	Prior Law	1997 Tax Act	Effective Date	Revenue Over 5 Years
84	Foreign Tax Credit Limitation for AMT Purposes	Separate limit used.	Simplified foreign tax credit limit may be elected.	Tax years beginning after 12/31/97.	<-$5 million
85	Foreign Tax Credit Limitation for 10/50 Company	Excess credits of a 10/50 company cannot offset income in other baskets.	Single credit limitation applies to all 10/50 companies.	Tax years beginning after 12/31/02.	-$982 million
86	Transfers to Foreign Corporations, Partnerships, Estates or Trusts	Inherent gain subject to excise tax rules.	Excise tax repealed; transfers trigger gain recognition.	Date of enactment.	(See below.)
86	Partnership Residence	A foreign partnership is one that is not domestic.	Treasury authorized to write regulations treating partnerships as foreign.	Partnerships created after regulations issued.	—
87	Controlled Foreign Corporation (CFC) Sale	Gain from CFC sale of lower tier CFC is Subpart F income to U.S. shareholder.	Gain treated as dividend to the extent of E&P to the U.S. shareholder.	Transactions after date of enactment.	-$33 million (includes basis adjustment and other provisions)

Page	Subject	Prior Law	1997 Tax Act	Effective Date	Revenue Over 5 Years
88	Stock Basis in CFC	No provision.	CFC's basis in its share of another CFC increased for undistributed previously taxed income to U.S. shareholder.	Tax years of U.S. shareholders beginning after 12/31/97.	(See above.)
88	CFC and Passive Foreign Investment Company (PFIC) Rules	U.S. CFC shareholder subject to Subpart F rules and PFIC interest charge rules.	Certain U.S. shareholders not subject to PFIC rules if overlap with Subpart F and PFIC rules.	Tax years beginning after 12/31/97.	-$124 million (election and other provisions)
88	PFIC Interest-charge Rules	No provision.	Rules avoided if U.S. shareholder elects mark-to-market for PFIC shares.	U.S. tax years beginning after 12/31/97.	(See above.)
90	CFC Acquisition	U.S. shareholder's Subpart F income reduced by actual dividends paid to other shareholder.	Also reduced by Sec. 1248 deemed dividend.	Acquisitions occurring after date of enactment.	Not available.
90	Foreign Personal Holding Company (FPHC) Income	Foreign passive income earned by foreign corporation is FPHC income.	Net income from notional principal contracts generally FPHC income.	Tax years beginning after date of enactment.	$92 million (other related provisions)

Page	Subject	Prior Law	1997 Tax Act	Effective Date	Revenue Over 5 Years
91	Contributions to Foreign Corporations	Contributed intangibles treated as sold in exchange for deemed U.S. source royalty payment from transferee.	Deemed royalty is foreign source income if actual payment qualifies.	Transfers made and royalties deemed received after date of enactment.	-$4 million (information reporting, repeal of excise tax and other provisions)
92	Foreign Partnership Information Reporting	U.S. return filed if U.S. source income or engaged in U.S. business.	Deductions, losses and credits not available if required returns not filed.	Tax years beginning after date of enactment.	(See above.)
92	Information Reporting for U.S. Partners and Transfers to Foreign Partnerships	U.S. persons acquiring/disposing of foreign partnership interest may have to report.	"Controlling" U.S. partners file information returns; certain transfers by U.S. transferor reportable.	Transfers occurring after date of enactment.	—
93	Information Reporting for Shareholders and Directors of Foreign Corporations	Information returns if 5% stock value held.	New threshold is 10% of the vote or value of foreign corporation's stock.	1/1/98	(See above.)

Page	Subject	Prior Law	1997 Tax Act	Effective Date	Revenue Over 5 Years
93	Sec. 911 Foreign Earned Income Exclusion	$70,000 U.S. expatriate annual maximum exclusion for foreign earned income.	Maximum increased to $80,000 in $2,000 increments beginning in 1998; indexed in 2006.	Tax years beginning after 12/31/97.	$244 million
94	Individual Foreign Tax Credit Limitation	Separate limitation rule applies; passive investment income taxes segregated from other income.	No limitation if no more than $300 ($600 joint) of creditable foreign taxes and election made.	Tax years beginning after 12/31/97.	$5 million
94	Foreign Currency Exchange	Individual taxable gain upon currency conversion to U.S. dollars.	Gains not exceeding $200 not taxed.	Tax years beginning after 12/31/97.	< -$5 million
95	Treaty Withholding Rates	Treaty benefits for lower withholding rates limited for U.S. or foreign hybrid.	Additional limits on treaty benefits for payments to hybrid entities.	Date of enactment.	$5 million

Pass-Through Entities

Page	Subject	Prior Law	1997 Tax Act	Effective Date	Revenue Over 5 Years
99	Multiple Property Distribution—Basis Allocation	Partner's basis in distributed non-cash property is based on partnership's basis in distributed assets	Certain property distributions consider appreciation/depreciation in property distributed.	Distributions after date of enactment.	$249 million
101	Partnership Inventory	Substantial inventory appreciation is ordinary income upon sale or exchange.	All inventory appreciation is ordinary income upon sale or exchange.	Property sales or exchanges and distributions after date of enactment; binding contracts effective 6/8/97 grandfathered.	$316 million
102	Pre-Contribution Gain	Contributing partner recognizes gain on certain distributions within five years.	Increased to seven years.	Contributions after 6/8/97; binding contracts grandfathered.	$2 million
103	Publicly Traded Partnerships	Taxed as corporations, but some partnership treatment grandfathered through 1997.	Grandfathered partnerships can make one-time election of 3.5% gross business income tax to retain partnership treatment.	Tax years beginning after 12/31/97.	—

Coopers & Lybrand L.L.P.

Page	Subject	Prior Law	1997 Tax Act	Effective Date	Revenue Over 5 Years
104	Electing Large Partnerships	All tax return items separately reported on Schedule K.	Only 11 items are reported.	Tax years beginning after 12/31/97.	$38 million
105	Deceased Partner	Partnership year does not close on partner's death.	Partnership year closes upon partner's death.	Tax years beginning after 12/31/97.	-$1 million
106	S Corporation ESOP Shareholders	S corporation income scheduled to become UBIT.	UBIT treatment repealed.	Tax years beginning after 12/31/97.	-$149 million
108	RIC 30% Gross Income Requirement	Limit on gains generated by mutual fund from sale of securities held less than 3 months.	Limit repealed.	Mutual fund tax years beginning after date of enactment.	-$138 million
108	RIC Trading Safe Harbor	Requires principal office outside U.S. for offshore corporations and partnerships trading on own account.	Requirement eliminated.	Tax years beginning after 12/31/97.	<-$0.5 million
108	REIT Shareholder Demand Letters	REIT disqualified where no effort to ascertain ownership.	Penalties replace disqualification; compliance satisfies closely-held ownership test.	Tax years beginning after date of enactment.	—

Page	Subject	Prior Law	1997 Tax Act	Effective Date	Revenue Over 5 Years
109	REIT Tenant Services	Impermissible service can disqualify tenant rent income.	*De minimis* impermissible service permitted.	Tax years beginning after date of enactment.	—
110	REIT Capital Gains Credit	Retained capital gains taxed to REIT and shareholder.	Shareholder credit for REIT-paid tax on retained capital gains.	Tax years beginning after date of enactment.	—
110	REIT 30% Gross Income Requirement	30% cap on income from certain sources.	Cap repealed.	Tax years beginning after date of enactment.	—
113	Small Partnership Audits	Partnership items determined at entity level, except small partnerships with 10 or fewer noncorporate partners.	Small partnership exclusion applies to partnerships with corporate partners.	Tax years ending after date of enactment.	-$3 million
113	Electing Large Partnerships	Partnership adjustments made to partner shares in year of examination.	Partnerships with 100 or more partners may elect to take partnership adjustments into account for computing partners' current-year shares of partnership items or pay imputed underpayment; prior-year returns unaffected; new information return requirements.	Tax years ending on or after December 31, 1997.	$2 million

Coopers & Lybrand L.L.P.

Page	Subject	Prior Law	1997 Tax Act	Effective Date	Revenue Over 5 Years
114	Partnerships with more than 100 partners	Filing on magnetic media permitted.	Magnetic media required.	Tax years ending on or after 12/31/97.	—
116	Corporate Tax Shelters	No registration required.	Promoter must submit identifying information and tax benefits to Treasury; penalties apply; special rules for foreign promoters.	Applies after IRS guidance issued.	$170 million
118	Individual Estimated Tax Underpayment Threshold	$500 threshold used to calculate estimated tax penalties.	Increased to $1,000.	Tax years beginning after 12/31/97.	-$208 million
118	Individual Estimated Tax Safe Harbor	If AGI over $150,000, no penalty if 110% of preceding year tax paid.	Threshold adjusted to 105% of preceding year tax for tax years beginning in 1999, 2000 and 2001; 112% for 2002; 110% thereafter.	Tax years beginning in 1999.	$1 billion
119	Payments to Attorneys	No provision.	Reportable on Form 1099-B if not otherwise reportable on Form 1099-MISC or W-2.	Payments after 12/31/97.	$12 million
119	Interest on Large Corporate Underpayments	Higher interest rate applies 30 days after first deficiency notice or letter of assessment.	Certain notices disregarded under provision increasing interest rate on large corporate underpayments.	Periods after 12/31/97.	-$5 million

Page	Subject	Prior Law	1997 Tax Act	Effective Date	Revenue Over 5 Years
119	EFTPS Penalty	No penalties through 1997 for failure to make electronic tax deposits.	Penalties delayed until July 1, 1998, if depositor not required to use EFTPS before 1997.	N/A	—
120	Substantial Understatement Penalty	Defines tax shelter; no specific exception for certain multi-party financing transactions.	Amended "tax shelter" definition; no reasonable basis exception for understatements resulting from certain multi-party financing transactions.	Transactions entered into after date of enactment.	$170 million
120	Reasonable Cause Exceptions	No provision.	Reasonable cause exceptions for failure to report deductible employee retirement plan contributions and certain small business stock information; to file a personal holding company tax return (for foreign corporations), to make certain payments (for fiscal year entities).	Tax years beginning after date of enactment.	—
121	Refund Claims Statute of Limitations	Refund claim must be filed within 3 years of filing return or 2 years from tax payment date.	Allows refund claims within three years of return due date even if no return filed, in certain circumstances.	Tax years ending after date of enactment.	—

Page	Subject	Prior Law	1997 Tax Act	Effective Date	Revenue Over 5 Years
121	Statute of Limitations— Pass-Throughs	No provision.	Statute runs on underpayments attributable to third-party distributions based on recipients' return filing date.	Tax years ending after date of enactment.	—
122	Securities Brokers	No provision.	Certain instructions to securities brokers ignored for worker classification purposes.	Services performed after 12/31/97.	—
125	Unrelated Business Income Tax	Certain sponsorship payments received by tax-exempt organization subject to UBIT.	Qualified corporate sponsorship payments exempt from UBIT.	Payments solicited or paid after 12/31/97.	—
125	Controlled Subsidiaries	Interest, rents and royalties from 80% directly controlled subsidiary taxed.	Threshold is 50% direct or indirect control.	Tax years beginning after date of enactment, except binding contracts effective 6/8/97.	$8 million
126	Tax-Exempt Bond Cap	$150 million limit on bonds issued by certain charitable organizations.	Lifts limit for bonds issued solely for capital expenditures.	Expenditures incurred after date of enactment.	-$315 million

Page	Subject	Prior Law	1997 Tax Act	Effective Date	Revenue Over 5 Years
126	Private Foundation Estimated Taxes	First quarter payment due April 15, if calendar year.	May 15 due date.	Tax years beginning after date of enactment.	-$2 million
126	Contribution of Appreciated Stock to Private Foundations	Deduct FMV of qualified appreciated stock contributed through 5/31/97.	Extends to 6/30/98.	6/1/97	-$112 million
126	Tax-Exempt Entity Proxy Tax	General disclosure requirements and proxy tax.	Exempt if 90% of aggregate annual dues are paid by tax-exempt entities, individuals or families whose annual dues are less than $100.	12/31/97	—
127	Charitable Mileage Deduction	12 cents per mile deduction.	Increases to 14 cents per mile.	Tax years beginning after 12/31/97.	-$247 million
129	Air Transportation "Ticket Tax"	10% excise tax for domestic; $6 per passenger on international departures; foreign arrivals not taxed.	Extended from 10/1/97 through 9/30/07; reduced to 7.5% by 10/1/99; applies to payments for frequent flyer miles; 7.5% for rural airports; foreign arrivals and departures generally taxed at $12; additional tax on domestic segment.	Transportation beginning after 9/30/97, with exceptions.	$25.8 billion

Coopers & Lybrand L.L.P.

Pensions

Page	Subject	Prior Law	1997 Tax Act	Effective Date	Revenue Over 5 Years
130	Communication Services	3% tax on communications services.	Applies to prepaid phone cards.	Payments more than 60 days after date of enactment.	$193 million
131	Environmental Excise Tax	Leaking Underground Storage Tank Trust Fund 0.1% per gallon tax on gasoline, diesel and special motor fuels.	Reinstated for the period 10/1/97 through 3/31/05.	10/1/97	$645 million
		Tax on ozone depleting chemicals.	Extends to imported recycled halon-1211.	Date of enactment.	$1 million
133	Section 401(k) Investments	Companies can mandate employee 401(k) investment in company stock.	10% limit on mandatory investment of elective deferrals.	Plan years beginning after 1998.	—
134	Excess Distribution Tax	15% excess distribution tax; 15% excise tax on certain retirement accumulations.	Both taxes repealed.	Distributions after 1996; deaths after 1996.	-$8 million
134	Excise Tax on Contributions	10% excise tax on nondeductible contributions; waiver available.	Waiver expanded.	Tax years beginning after 12/31/97.	-$14 million

Page	Subject	Prior Law	1997 Tax Act	Effective Date	Revenue Over 5 Years
134	Lump Sum Cashouts	Pension plans can cash out employees with $3,500 lump sums.	Limit increased to $5,000.	Plan years beginning after date of enactment.	$22.5 million
135	Government Plans	Qualification rules apply, such as participation and testing rules.	Most rules inapplicable.	Tax years beginning on or after date of enactment.	—

List of Coopers & Lybrand Offices

Albany, New York
Steve C. Appe
518-462-2030

Atlanta, Georgia
Jonathan J. Davies
404-870-1100

Austin, Texas
Francis J. Reeves
512-477-1300

Baltimore, Maryland
Frederick W. Haas
410-783-7600

Birmingham, Alabama
Thomas Lee
205-252-8400

Boise, Idaho
Thayne Maas
208-343-4801

Boston, Massachusetts
Michael J. Costello
617-478-5000

Charlotte, North Carolina
George W. Rohe
704-375-8414

Chicago, Illinois
Frank J. Gaudio
312-701-5500

Cincinnati, Ohio
Michael E. Braun
513-651-4000

Cleveland, Ohio
Scott D. Brackett
216-241-4380

Columbus, Ohio
Everett E. Gallagher, Jr.
614-225-8700

Dallas, Texas
J. Scott Duncan
214-754-5000

Dayton, Ohio
Michael E. Braun
513-223-5185

Denver, Colorado
Randy Stein
303-573-2800

Detroit, Michigan
Matthew J. Rizik
313-446-7100

El Paso, Texas
Luigi A. Pereira
915-545-5800

Eugene, Oregon
Lynn K. Schoenfeld
503-485-1600

Fort Lauderdale, Florida
Ricardo Gonzalez
305-764-7111

Fort Myers, Florida
Steven M. Appel
813-433-0888

Ft. Wayne, Indiana
William M. Gerke
219-423-1531

Fort Worth, Texas
Michael R. Baylor
817-332-2243

Grand Rapids, Michigan
David A. Wilson
616-458-7700

Greensboro, North Carolina
Mark D. Yarbrough
910-691-1000

Harrisburg, Pennsylvania
David W. Zimmerman
717-231-5900

Hartford, Connecticut
Robert D. Batch
203-241-7000

Honolulu, Hawaii
Joseph H. Goldcamp, III
808-531-3400

Houston, Texas
W. Keith Booth
713-757-5200

Indianapolis, Indiana
Kevin P. Crowe
317-639-4161

Jacksonville, Florida
Sherrie Winokur
904-354-0671

Kansas City, Missouri
John Martin
816-474-6800

Knoxville, Tennessee
Carole Belmar
615-524-4000

Lexington, Kentucky
Laura D. Wigglesworth
606-255-3366

Lincoln, Nebraska
Bruce A. Hocking
402-475-7633

Long Island, New York (Melville)
John P. Lane
516-753-2700

Los Angeles, California
John A. Sandmeier
213-356-6000

Louisville, Kentucky
Ronald W. Abrams
502-589-6100

Maui, Hawaii (Wailuku)
Joseph H. Goldcamp, III
808-244-5527

Memphis, Tennessee
Max W. Piwonka
901-529-1100

Miami, Florida
Ricardo Gonzalez
305-375-7400

Milwaukee, Wisconsin
Robert C. Goldie
414-271-3200

Minneapolis, Minnesota
John L. Clymer
612-370-9300

Montgomery, Alabama
Thomas J. Lee, Jr.
205-834-9107

New Orleans, Louisiana
David R. Hoffman
504-529-2700

Newport Beach, California
Douglas S. Myers
714-251-7200

Newport News, Virginia
Joseph G. Robbins, Jr.
804-873-0030

New York, New York
Jesse Sprecher
212-259-1000

Oklahoma City, Oklahoma
Paul Brou
405-236-5800

Omaha, Nebraska
John R. Uhrich
402-344-4545

Orlando, Florida
Mark F. Johnson
407-843-1190

Parsippany, New Jersey
Donald J. Scotto
201-829-9000

Philadelphia, Pennsylvania
Robert C. Morris
215-963-8000

Phoenix, Arizona
Russ McQueen
602-280-1800

Pittsburgh, Pennsylvania
Dave Lancia
412-355-8000

Portland, Maine
Gain S. Francis
207-791-5200

Portland, Oregon
Michael D. Weber
503-227-8600

Raleigh, North Carolina
Arthur Guy
919-755-3000

Richmond, Virginia
James B. Grow
804-697-1900

Rochester, New York
John A. Thorne
716-263-7200

Sacramento, California
Jon V. Martin
916-441-4334

St. Louis, Missouri
Daniel R. Schultz
314-436-3200

Salt Lake City, Utah
Scott W. Pickett
801-531-9666

San Diego, California
Walter D. Alexander
619-525-2300

San Francisco, California
David L. Millstein
415-957-3000

Coopers & Lybrand L.L.P.

San Jose, California
Glen L. Rossman
408-295-1020

San Juan, Puerto Rico
Charles Rosario
809-756-6050

Seattle, Washington
Constance E. Skidmore
206-622-8700

South Bend, Indiana
Kenneth J. Keber
219-234-4021

Spartanburg, South Carolina
William V. Kastler
803-573-1097

Spokane, Washington
Richard W. Beebe
509-455-9300

Springfield, Massachusetts
Richard J. Callahan
413-781-7200

Stamford, Connecticut
Kenneth L. Maxon
203-326-8400

Syracuse, New York
John E. Reynolds
315-474-8541

Tampa, Florida
Brett Hendee
813-229-0221

Tulsa, Oklahoma
Jack E. Short
918-596-8200

Virginia Beach, VA
Joseph G. Robbins, Jr.
804-497-1400

Washington, D.C. (McLean, VA)
Fernando Murias
703-918-3000

West Palm Beach, Florida
William F. Fong
407-832-0038

U.S. Tax Representatives Abroad

Brussels, Belgium
James E. Harris
2-774-4211

Mexico City, Mexico
Manuel Solano
5-208-1277

Tokyo, Japan
Dean A. Yoost
3-5563-8211

London, United Kingdom
Pamela Jackson
71-583-5000